THE MANATEE

Look for these and other books in the
Lucent Endangered Animals and Habitats Series:

The Amazon Rain Forest
The Bald Eagle
The Bear
The Elephant
The Giant Panda
The Gorilla
The Manatee
The Oceans
The Rhinoceros
Seals and Sea Lions
The Shark
The Tiger
The Whale
The Wolf

Other related titles in the Lucent Overview Series:

Acid Rain
Endangered Species
Energy Alternatives
Garbage
The Greenhouse Effect
Hazardous Waste
Ocean Pollution
Oil Spills
Ozone
Pesticides
Population
Rainforests
Recycling
Saving the American Wilderness
Vanishing Wetlands
Zoos

THE MANATEE

BY CLAIRE PRICE-GROFF

Endangered Animals & Habitats

LUCENT BOOKS, INC.
SAN DIEGO, CALIFORNIA

LUCENT Overview Series

I would like to thank Dr. Gregory Bossart, Wayne Hartley, Ann Perry, Jim Reid, Nancy Sadusky, Ann Spellman, Bob Turner, Leslie Ward, Ross Wilcox, and all of the people who so generously gave me their time and expertise in the preparation of this book.

Library of Congress Cataloging-in-Publication Data

Price-Groff, Claire.
    The manatee / Claire Price-Groff.
       p.   cm. — (Endangered animals & habitats)
    Includes bibliographical references (p.   ) and index.
    Summary: Discusses the physical characteristics, behavior, habitats, and endangered status of the manatee and the closely related dugong.
    ISBN 1-56006-445-5 (lib. bdg. : alk. paper)
    1. Sirenia—Juvenile literature.   2. Endangered species—Juvenile literature. [1. Manatees. 2. Endangered species.] I. Title. II. Series.
    QL737.S6P75   1999
    599.55—dc21   98-53230
                                            CIP
                                              AC

*To Howard
and
the future of manatees and dugongs*

Contents

Introduction

OF ALL THE sea mammals, the sirenians—manatees and their cousin dugongs—attract the least amount of attention from humans. There are no *Free Willy*–type movies featuring manatees or dugongs, and only very seldom are they featured on the many nature programs shown on television. They are never the stars of marine park shows. They are not flamboyant show-offs like dolphins. They don't jump through hoops or balance balls on their noses. They are large, but not of the gargantuan proportions of whales. They do not have large soulful eyes like baby seals. And they don't harrumph and bellow their claims to territory like sea lions.

But these little-known and often misunderstood animals are fascinating and well worth knowing. In spite of their large size, they are completely harmless to both man and other animals. When in the vicinity of humans, they exhibit an appealing curiosity and even affection.

It wasn't so long ago that the only people who were familiar with manatees and dugongs were either scientists who studied them or people who lived along the coastlines they inhabit. And for most of the world's history, those people hunted manatees and dugongs for their delicious meat, leatherlike hides, oil, and bones. As with whales and seals, the hunting was taking its toll, and the numbers of animals were diminishing. No one thought about the extinction of an entire species.

In the natural course of evolution, it takes hundreds of centuries for a species to become extinct. Occasionally over the millions of years of the earth's history, a cataclysmic event such as the collision of an extremely large asteroid or comet with the earth has led to sudden dramatic changes in the earth's contours and in its climate. These changes in turn are thought to have contributed to the extinction of certain species, as is suspected in the case of the dinosaurs. But when humans hunt an animal relentlessly or interfere drastically with its environment, a species can become extinct in a matter of years, as happened with one species of Sirenia only a couple of hundred years ago.

In the 1960s, Rachel Carson's book, *Silent Spring,* shocked the world into awareness of the importance of conservation. It was the first serious look at the damage human intervention was causing to the world's natural environment. Carson warned that if humans did not change their way of interacting with nature, not only might a few species become extinct, but the entire world would be at risk.

Though their large size may make them look threatening, manatees are in fact harmless to other marine animals and humans.

Conservation and changing perceptions

The ultimate goal of conservation is to foster conditions that will increase populations that are endangered to the point where they are able to maintain themselves for now and far into the future. According to Sidney J. Holt and Lee M. Talbot, two leading conservationists, conservation includes

> management measures, and means the collection and application of biological information for the purposes of increasing and maintaining the number of animals within species and populations at some optimum level with respect to their habitat. Used in this way, conservation refers to the entire scope of activities that constitute a modern scientific resource program, including research, census, law enforcement, habitat acquisition and improvement, and periodic or total protection as well as regulated taking.[1]

Studies on the Florida manatee

Before conservation measures can be taken for any particular animal, knowledge about that animal's lifestyle, needs, and habitat must be gathered. Though some studies were done on injured manatees brought to the Miami Seaquarium in the 1950s, much of what is known today about manatees and other sirenians is based on Daniel S. Hartman's book, *Ecology and Behavior of the Manatee (Trichechus Manatus) in Florida.* Published in 1979, the book was a result of Hartman's long-term study of Florida manatees at the Crystal River hot springs, located on the west coast of Florida, approximately sixty miles north of Tampa. In recent years, marine and plant biologists, veterinarians, and other scientists around the world have added to Hartman's study, not only of the Florida manatee, but of Sirenia around the world. As with any ongoing research, new information is constantly being added to our knowledge about sirenians—and there is still much we do not know about them.

Since more is known about the Florida manatee than other sirenians, much of the information in this book refers to that species, but the information is largely applicable to

all other manatees and to dugongs as well. In cases where this is not so, specific information on other species of Sirenia is given.

The hot springs at Florida's Crystal River are host to manatees and the tourists and scientists who come to observe and study them.

Sirenians still in trouble

Though much has been written over the past decade about sirenians and the need to protect them, they are still in danger. Each year there are many deaths due to human interference in their world. The Florida manatee, especially, is victim to boating accidents. Manatees and dugongs in other parts of the world are still hunted for their meat. All sirenians are adversely affected by increasing human population growth and the consequent development of the coastal areas manatees frequent.

Human responsibility

Humans have the ability to change the world, both for better and for worse. Human exploitation of the earth's resources and natural wildlife habitats has resulted in the devastation and pollution of many coastal, river, and forest environments.

Science has proven that all life and environmental systems on earth are interconnected. One of the main challenges facing people today is finding a balance between satisfying current human needs and maintaining the earth, its air, and its water so that they will continue to support life in the future.

John E. Reynolds and Daniel K. Odell say, "Though manatees are rare and are affected by a variety of human activities, they show an adaptability and a toughness that suggest that, given half a chance, Florida manatees may survive better than many people might suspect."[2] Though they are speaking specifically of the Florida manatee, their words apply to all sirenians.

Positive signs

Through the work of several conservation organizations and through increased public awareness, there are some encouraging signs for the future of sirenians. The population of the Florida manatee seems to be gradually increasing. Other countries are studying their sirenian populations and making more of an effort to protect their habitats and to enforce worldwide restrictions against uncontrolled hunting. With continued awareness and diligence in protecting sirenians, they will be a part of our world for many centuries to come.

1

Manatees—Gentle Giants of the Sea

It's HARD TO imagine anyone mistaking a manatee for a mermaid. But in 1493, when Columbus's ships were taking on fresh water at the island known as Hispaniola, shared today by Haiti and the Dominican Republic, he recorded in his journal that his men "saw three sirenas (mermaids) who rose very high from the sea, but they were not as beautiful as they are painted."[3] It is generally agreed that the creatures were manatees.

Columbus and his men were not the only ones to mistake manatees, or their close cousins, dugongs, for mermaids. Writer Tim Dietz tells of the French priest Père Labat, who in 1732, reported on a captured "mermaid" in Africa. Labat's description could easily have been that of a dugong: a creature possessing a humanlike upper body with two breasts and two short arms [flippers], and a lower body of a fish with a long, forked tail.

Neither mermaids nor fish

Not everyone mistook manatees and dugongs for mermaids. Many people thought the creatures were huge fish. But they are neither mermaids nor fish. Both manatees and dugongs are mammals that belong to the scientific order Sirenia. Like all sea mammals, they must rise above the surface of the water to breathe air into their lungs. Sirenians are tropical animals that must live in waters at or above sixty-eight degrees Fahrenheit. They can live in either salt

Manatees and Greek Mythology

The association between mermaids, manatees, and dugongs remains today thanks to the nineteenth-century taxonomist (a scientist specializing in naming and classifying species) who chose Sirenia as the official name for the scientific order under which manatees and dugongs are classified. Sirens are another name for mermaids. In ancient Greek mythology the sirens were beautiful half-fish, half-women who sang haunting melodies that lured sailors to crash their boats on the rocks.

This ancient Greek carving depicts a siren using a horn to draw sailors toward her rocky lair.

water or freshwater, but scientists believe that manatees must, at least occasionally, find fresh water to drink. Manatees near boating docks are often observed drinking from water hoses. Dugongs, however, spend their entire lives in salt water. Experts believe the dugongs' kidneys have the ability to filter salt from their food, so they apparently have no need for freshwater.

More than just blobs in the sea

At first glance, these huge mammals look most like big, shapeless blobs floating beneath the surface of the water. When resting on the bottom, which they frequently do, sirenians can easily be mistaken for large rocks. Their bodies are oval shaped with no discernible neck, so their heads appear to be bulbous extensions of their upper bodies. A pair of short front flippers are used for locomotion and for manipulating food into their mouths. Daniel Hartman, who made the first long-term study of manatees, noted that "the flippers are held in close to the chest while swimming, but they are [also] used in 'walking' on the bottom."[4] Females have teats just under their flippers.

Though all species of Sirenia are similar, there are some major differences between them. The manatee's body is rotund, narrowing slightly before it flares into a broad, paddle-shaped tail. The dugong's body is more streamlined, tapering gradually into the tail, which flares out into two flukes (like a dolphin's). The manatee has rough, wrinkled skin that is brownish gray in color, while the dugong has smooth skin that is dark gray on the topside and light gray on the underside. The manatee's lips are very large and the upper

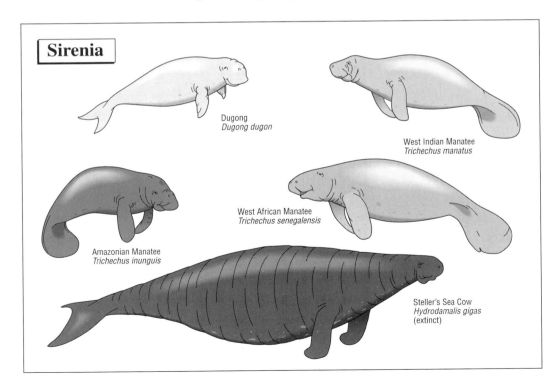

Sirenia

Dugong
Dugong dugon

West Indian Manatee
Trichechus manatus

West African Manatee
Trichechus senegalensis

Amazonian Manatee
Trichechus inunguis

Steller's Sea Cow
Hydrodamalis gigas
(extinct)

lip is divided so each side can move independently to push food into its mouth. The dugong's upper snout is also divided, with each side capable of independent movement, but its lower snout slants downwards, ending in a flattened area called the rostral disk. This disk is used to dig up rhizomes (underground plant growth) and roots from the sea bottom. Most species of manatees have a feature unique to sea mammals— three or four fingernails at the ends of the flippers. And dugongs have small tusks that erupt through the upper jaw at around nine or ten years of age. All sirenians have very sparse body hair and long whiskers on either side of the snout.

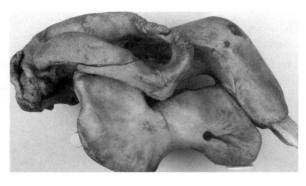

This dugong skull shows the rostral disk, which the animal uses to scoop food from the seabed.

Manatees can grow as long as thirteen feet and weigh up to thirty-five hundred pounds, although the average is ten feet long and weighs around twelve hundred pounds. Dugongs are somewhat smaller, with the average adult reaching a length of nine and one-half feet and weighing around nine hundred pounds.

Sirenian senses

Contrary to earlier belief, sirenian senses are well developed. Although their external ear openings are either not present at all or are very tiny, their internal ear bones are large and they are thought to hear well. Tests have determined that they are able to hear sounds at lower frequencies than humans can. Some scientists think that sound reception is located near the large cheekbones that are in direct contact with the ear bones rather than the tiny ear openings. This arrangement is similar to that of dolphins, "in which it is theorized that sound enters the fat-filled lower jaw and is conducted to the ear bones, apparently bypassing the tiny ear canal."[5]

Because sirenian eyes are tiny and set deep and wide apart, it used to be thought that they had poor eyesight. However, more rigorous testing has determined that they can see well in both dim and bright light and may see color, but their vision may sometimes be limited because of the murkiness of the water in which they swim.

They seem to have a fairly well-developed sense of smell, which scientists think they use to recognize one another and for males to know when a female is in estrus (ready to mate). A sense of taste is demonstrated by their preferences for certain plants. Their sense of touch is also highly acute and is one of the sirenians' most important senses.

Special adaptations

Because they live in the water rather than on land, sirenians have developed a number of special adaptations. Manatee nostrils have a special membrane that opens above the water and closes when the animal submerges. The dugong's nostrils do not close, but internal muscles contract to close the passage when the animal is submerged. Both manatees and dugongs have built-in eye protection in the form of nictitating membranes, transparent tissue that covers the eyeballs, enabling the animals to swim with their eyes open. Another adaptation to their aquatic environment is the sirenians' ability to replace 90 percent of the air in their lungs in one breath, thus enabling them to remain submerged for up to fifteen to twenty minutes at a time. By comparison, humans can only replace 10 percent of the air in their lungs with each breath.

Sirenians are unusual, as well, in their ability to rise vertically to the surface and sink back down again, like a helicopter or an elevator. The animals rise straight up, breathe, then sink straight down. There are no muscle or body movements during these surfacings. Scientists think sirenians can do this because their bones lack marrow, a soft connective tissue that is filled with air pockets. This lack of marrow makes the bones extremely dense and heavy. Reynolds and Odell, in their book, *Manatees and Dugongs,* suggest that the heavy bones "may have a very important function as ballast to offset the [animal's] positive buoyancy [tendency to float]."[6]

Marching teeth

Another special manatee adaptation, related to their diet of fibrous grasses and plants, was the subject of a paper published by Daryl Domning when this world-renowned expert was studying Amazonian manatees in 1975. It was always known that sirenians have thick, ridged pads instead of front teeth and that the ridges help to break vegetation into small pieces that are then pushed to the back of the mouth where the chewing molars are located. This rough diet, plus the grit that is often mixed with it, wears down the molars quite regularly. Domning explained that as a manatee's rear teeth wear down, they move to the front and fall out. As the old teeth fall out, new molars grow to replace them. Only manatees have these "marching teeth." Dugongs' teeth do not replace themselves. Once a dugong's original molars wear out, the roots remain in place, forming smooth pegs that function as teeth—though not very efficient ones.

Evolution of sirenia

These adaptations have come about over millions of years. Scientists believe that sirenians evolved around fifty-five million years ago from small, hoofed animals. Though

Instead of front teeth, a manatee has thick, ridged pads that it uses to break apart its food. Molars in the back of the mouth finish the job.

Along with the elephant, the hyrax (pictured) is the closest living relative of the manatee.

it seems unlikely, their closest living relatives today are elephants and small Asian mammals called hyraxes. Although there are vast differences between elephants, hyraxes, and sirenians, fossil evidence shows that all three evolved from a common ancestor. The manatees' toenails, skin color and texture, the absence of body hair, and the shape of their skulls are visible remnants of their ancient heritage. The dugongs' tusks are another link to elephants. And like elephants, sirenians are enormous animals.

Today, there are five species of Sirenia, but scientists believe that there were many more in the past. Early forms of manatees are thought to have originated near the Amazon basin in South America. Some remained there to become the Amazonian manatee (*Trichechus inunguis*), while others migrated up through the Caribbean, giving rise to the Antillean (*Trichechus manatus manatus*) and Florida manatees (*Trichechus manatus latirostris*). Another group managed to swim or were carried on currents across the Atlantic and became the West African manatee (*Trichechus senegalensis*).

Dugongs, known by the scientific name as *Dugong dugong,* are thought to have evolved along with manatees, and they once ranged from Europe to Africa, and along the east and west coasts of the Americas. At the present time, they are found only in the Eastern Hemisphere in the Indian and Pacific Oceans. Steller's sea cow, another species of Sirenia, became extinct in the 1700s.

Dwindling populations

Several thousand years ago, manatees were plentiful along the coasts of northern South America, the Caribbean Sea, and the southeast coast of Florida. Today in all areas, the numbers of manatees are vastly diminished.

Manatees, which at the time were not known in Europe, might have been a new sight to Columbus's men, but the

 ### Twelve-Million-Year-Old Manatee

Fossil bones from around the world are physical proof that sirenians have existed for millions of years. In 1963 the fossilized skeleton of a large sea creature was uncovered in a sand quarry in California. The creature turned out to be a prehistoric sirenian, more like a dugong than a manatee, approximately ten to twelve million years old, which lived in the bays and inland seas that existed at that time in California. Like modern sirenians, this creature, which scientists named *Dusisiren jordani,* fed on algae and sea grasses.

The bones are kept at the University of California at Berkeley, but a plastic replica, cast from the original bones, is on display at the Santa Cruz Museum of Natural History in Santa Cruz, California.

This reproduction of a fossilized manatee found in a California sand quarry is on exhibit in Santa Cruz.

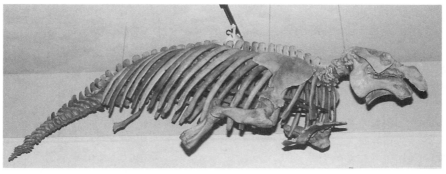

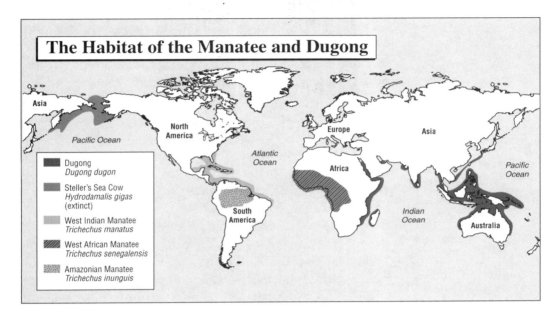

The Habitat of the Manatee and Dugong

Dugong
Dugong dugon

Steller's Sea Cow
Hydrodamalis gigas
(extinct)

West Indian Manatee
Trichechus manatus

West African Manatee
Trichechus senegalensis

Amazonian Manatee
Trichechus inunguis

natives who lived on the islands were well acquainted with this animal, which they hunted for both its meat and its hide. Soon after Columbus's arrival, other European explorers and settlers arrived in the New World, and they, too, began hunting the manatee. The dugong has also been a victim of thousands of years of hunting.

Sirenians have no defense mechanisms. Their only means of protection is to swim away from whatever is threatening them. They have few natural enemies, although the Amazonian manatees are occasionally prey to jaguars and caimans, a type of crocodile. And dugongs are sporadically attacked by sharks. Today, the biggest threat to all sirenians is from humans. All but the Florida manatee are still hunted. All are losing habitat to increased human activity and development of coastal areas. And all fall victim to human-related activities such as being caught in large gill nets or shark nets—or colliding with boats.

Dugongs

Of the currently existing species of Sirenia, the one with the largest population is the dugong, which swims in the waters of the Indian Ocean, eastern Africa, the Red Sea, the Persian and Arabian Gulfs, southern Asia, the Philippines, Borneo, New Guinea, and Australia. The numbers vary in different locations from under a hundred to several thousand, but in all areas there are far fewer than there were just ten years ago. According to Masaharu Nishiwaki and Helene Marsh, who conducted an extensive study of dugongs in 1985, "The precise extent to which the dugong's range has been contracted is unknown, but over much of its present range it is now represented by relict [remnant] populations separated by large areas where it is close to extinction or extinct."[7]

The largest concentrations of dugongs today are found off the coast of northern Australia in the waters of the Great Barrier Reef. According to Tony Stokes, the coordinator of the threatened species of the Great Barrier Reef Marine Park Authority, "The population is in serious decline in the southern Great Barrier Reef, down by 50–80 percent over the last twenty years."[8] As of early 1998, though dugongs in Australia were not classified as endangered, they were classified as vulnerable, meaning that they are close to becoming endangered. They are listed as endangered throughout the remainder of their range.

Florida and Antillean manatees

The Florida manatee, which makes its home in the waters of the southeastern and gulf waters of the United States, and the Antillean manatee, which swims in the Caribbean Sea around the countries of Central America and northeastern South America, are quite similar. Until 1986 they were considered one species known as the West Indian manatee (*Trichechus manatus*). The differences are in the shape of their skulls and other minor anatomical features. "It was not until the 1980s that sufficient anatomical material was available to allow scientists to confirm the subspecies distinction on the basis of skull characteristics."[9] The 1997 counts of the Florida manatee indicate between two thousand and twenty-five hundred animals.

Because the Antillean manatee swims in the waters of many different countries and changes locations in the rainy

Sirenian Names

The name manatee derives from the Spanish *manati,* which is believed to have come from the Carib word *manattou,* and means "woman's breast." The Caribs were a native tribe living in the West Indies at the time of Columbus. The word "dugong" is derived from *duyong,* the Malaysian word for these animals.

Both manatees and dugongs are often called sea cows because they graze on sea grasses and plants. In Brazil, the Amazonian manatee is often called *piese-boi,* or ox-fish. Dugongs, which feed by rooting on the bottom of the sea, are often called sea pigs, pigfish, water pig, or digging pig. In South Africa, the Afrikaans name for dugong is *nijlpaar*—a Dutch word for hippopotamus. In the United Arab Emirates, dugongs are known as *Aroos al-Bahar,* Bride of the Sea, or *Baghr al-Bahr,* sea cow.

Manatees and dugongs are frequently called sea cows because they graze on sea grass.

season, often seeking out remote regions, it has been difficult to accurately assess its total population. It is known, however, that its numbers have decreased drastically.

Amazonian and West African manatees

Little research has been done on the Amazonian and West African manatees. The Amazonian manatee, the only one to live completely in freshwater, inhabits the rivers and estuaries of the Orinoco and Amazon River basins in northern South America. As with the Antillean manatee, it has been difficult to determine exact numbers of these species, but again it is known that the population is much reduced from fifty to sixty years ago. At one time there were huge herds of Amazonian manatees; today there are only small groups of four to eight animals.

In some areas, the West African manatee has become extinct.

Protecting sirenians around the world

Because of the shrinking of sirenian populations, international conservation organizations and individual countries have included them among protected species. All species of Sirenia are listed under the U.S. Endangered Species Act, passed by Congress in 1973. That act states that a species is endangered if it is in danger of extinction in all or a large part of its natural habitat. The act makes it a violation to harass or in any way harm endangered species. The World Conservation Union's Red Data Books, which classifies species as endangered (likely to become extinct under current conditions), vulnerable (likely to become endangered under current conditions), or rare (uncommon, but not in imminent danger) lists all manatees and dugongs as vulnerable. The Convention on International Trade in Endangered Species of Wild Fauna and Flora (CITES)—an agreement among 103 countries for the regulation of trade in plants and animals that are or may be threatened with extinction—lists all dugongs outside of Australia and the Amazonian, Florida, and Antillean manatees as threatened with extinction. Dugongs

within Australian waters and the West African manatee are registered as vulnerable. The West African manatee is also protected by the African Convention of Nature and Natural Resources, and all other countries in which sirenians live have protective laws as well. In addition to these listings, the Florida manatee is also listed under other protective acts. But despite all this protection, many manatees and dugongs are killed each year.

Efforts to educate the public about the manatee's plight have included the issuing of commemorative postage stamps.

2

Sirenian Behavior

ANY SPECIES WHOSE death rate is higher than its birth rate is in danger of extinction. Since 1976 the death rate of Florida manatees has grown nearly 6 percent each year while the population has only grown at 2 to 4 percent each year. Precise birth and death statistics are not known for other sirenian species, but it is clear that all sirenian populations are declining.

For humans to help preserve any animal population, it is essential to know as much as possible about that animal's life cycle and behavior. And precisely for that reason, intense studies of manatee and dugong life must continue. Most of the information on sirenian behavior in this chapter is derived from studies on Florida manatees, but it is likely that other sirenian species follow similar patterns.

Part of the problem of maintaining viable sirenian populations is the animals' slow reproductive rate. Giving birth to a manatee or a dugong is a long, slow process. Each pregnancy, or gestation, lasts twelve to fourteen months. A sirenian produces only one calf every two to four years. Twins do occur, but rarely, and when they do, the babies are likely to be undersized and at greater risk than a single calf.

Sirenian births

Just as giving birth to a manatee is a long, slow process, so is caring for one and bringing it to maturity. As with any animal born in the wild, the first few months of life are precarious. Young sirenians, like young humans, have few natural instincts. They must learn what they need to know from their mothers. If the mother of a young calf is killed, it is very likely that the calf, too, will soon die. Sirenian mothers and calves form strong bonds and the calf remains by its mother's side until it is able to fend for itself—a period of three or more years.

A manatee calf is around forty-seven inches long at birth and weighs around sixty-six pounds. Almost immediately the newborn calf makes little squeaks and squeals, to which the mother responds. These sounds help to establish communication between mother and baby. The calf is able to swim by itself as soon as it emerges from the mother's womb, and within seconds of birth, it rises to the surface to breathe. Sometimes, though, the mother sets the baby on her back and rises to the surface, breathing then sinking. The reason for this behavior is unknown. The baby, which nurses underwater, begins suckling within a few hours of birth and within a few weeks, starts nibbling on plants.

A manatee and her week-old calf. Manatees are able to swim at birth.

Sirenian mothers and their young

When it is very young, the baby swims alongside its mother just behind her flipper. This arrangement may assist the baby in feeding or swimming because the baby experiences less drag from the water in that position. Also, this position

Lifespan and Length of Reproductivity

Scientists once thought that manatees did not reach sexual maturity until nine or ten years of age, but later studies and closer observations of animals in the wild have shown that females can become pregnant as young as three to five years old. Researchers still believe that dugongs are nine or ten years old at their first pregnancy.

No one knows how long a manatee remains capable of becoming pregnant, but Juliet, a captive manatee at Miami Seaquarium, gave birth to a calf in 1990 when she was between forty-four and forty-eight years old. Manatees live to be over fifty, and dugongs to over seventy.

An infant calf nurses just behind its mother's flipper. When not feeding, a manatee calf remains close to its mother so that the two can communicate.

enables mother and calf to touch one another, which, along with chirps, whistles, and squeaks, is how the two communicate. Wayne Hartley, who has been the ranger in charge of manatees at Blue Springs State Park, near Orlando, Florida, for over twenty years, says, "They have different whistles for different occasions: when they are scared, a mother calling a calf, or 'go away, don't bother me.'"[10]

Vocalizing is an especially important means of communication between mothers and their young. This was demonstrated when manatee rescuers were called in to free a mother and baby, both of which were trapped in a closed canal near the Miami international airport. The rescuers had little trouble capturing the baby with a net, but the mother was more elusive. After many tries, the rescuers tied the baby to a stake in a shallow part of the canal. As expected, the baby chirped and squeaked, and the mother came swimming to its side. The rescuers were then able to capture the adult female and place her and the calf into the river adjacent to the canal.

In another instance, observers watched a mother mana-tee that was separated from her baby by a partly opened floodgate. The strong current prevented the calf from swimming back to its mother, and the small opening in the gate kept the mother from swimming through. For three hours, the mother placed her head near the opening of the gate and called to her baby. At the next scheduled gate opening, the two were reunited.

Like most mothers, sirenians are defensive of their ba-bies; however, since these animals are totally nonaggres-sive, a sirenian mother will not fight to protect her calf. Instead, she places herself between the calf and the in-truder or swims away, knowing the calf will follow.

Wayne Hartley says manatee mothers are not unlike hu-man mothers. Some allow their young quite a bit of free-dom to explore, while others do not. Manatee mothers have been seen slapping calves with their flippers and sometimes even sitting on them, apparently to discipline them or to teach their calves correct behavior. Calves, too, exhibit different personalities. Some are adventuresome and wander off on their own, while others are more cau-tious and remain at their mothers' sides. But always, the calf returns to its mother, and the two feed together.

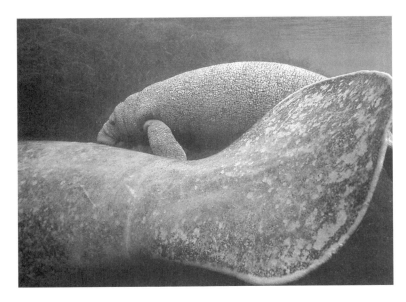

Manatee mothers some-times use their immense tails to discipline their young.

Young sirenians learn where to look for food and which plants are most desirable by watching and imitating their mothers. By the time it is an adult, the animal will consume between 5 and 11 percent of its body weight each day. A study conducted by the U.S. Fish and Wildlife Service at Crystal River in Florida, found that some manatees consumed over 15 percent of their body weight each day. That means a fifteen-hundred-pound animal eats up to 225 pounds of food a day. That's a lot of plants. To accomplish this formidable task, manatees spend up to eight hours a day feeding.

Sirenian diet choices

To the casual observer sirenians seem indiscriminate in their choice of plants for food, but they do have preferences. Manatees have been observed hauling themselves up on river or canal banks to eat fallen acorns. John Reynolds and Daniel Odell, who studied manatee feeding habits, say, "Manatees in Florida have been known to feed on over 60 species of plants, but they do avoid certain plants, such as some blue-green algae, that contain natural toxins."[11] Also, manatees in captivity show a definite preference to some plants over others.

Manatees sometimes drag themselves onto dry land to feed on grasses and acorns.

Sea Grasses and Sirenians

Sea grasses, which are like underwater flowering meadows, are feeding grounds for many species of invertebrates. They also provide refuge for fish during strong tides. Sea grass beds help to stabilize sea-bottom sediment through their root systems much as land plants on hillsides help to prevent erosion.

The availability of sea grasses is crucial to maintaining a manatee population large enough to assure its survival. But when people develop coastal areas, they often dredge canals and inlet bottoms. This not only tears up existing sea grass but loosens and frees the sediment. The water becomes murky, allowing less sunlight to filter through to the underwater plants, which inhibits their growth. Once a sea grass bed is destroyed, it seldom recovers.

For both manatees and dugongs, freshwater and sea grasses are overwhelmingly their favorite food and the mainstay of their diet. For that reason, favorite manatee feeding areas are the shallow, brackish water in inlets, rivers, and canals where sea grasses grow. Dugongs feed in shallow sea water where sea grasses are abundant.

During cold weather manatees take refuge in warm water springs and in areas around power plants. Since very few plants grow in these areas, the animals must travel up to twenty miles away to find available food. Rather than make this trip every day, many manatees will alter their usual feeding behavior. Instead of spending six to eight hours a day eating, they fast for a day and feed double the next day.

Amazonian manatees that seek out deeper waters during the dry season face a more severe problem. Once they are in these deep-water rivers, they no longer have access to the areas where most of their food grows. So they go with little or no food for the entire dry season, which can be as long as three or four months. Some of the Amazonian manatees eat any dead vegetable matter they find. This provides little nutrition and often makes the animals ill.

Others do not eat anything during these months. By the end of each dry season, many Amazonian manatees have died from malnutrition. Those that survive migrate to deep water where plants are more abundant, find food, and replenish their body fat for another year.

Swimming and diving

Since they favor shallow water, Florida manatees are under constant threat of being struck by powerboats.

Florida manatees' preference for shallow water is one of the reasons they are so often struck by boats or boat propellers. Ann Perry, of Florida's Department of Environmental Protection, says,

Many people think manatees are hit by boats because they are too slow, clumsy, or dumb to swim away. This is not so. Though they usually maintain a languid pace of swimming, they are capable of bursts of speed up to 15 miles an hour if they sense they are in danger. The reason they are hit is because of their size and bulk, there is simply no room for them to dive deeply enough or turn to get out of the way.[12]

In spite of their immense bulk, and their difficulty in escaping slashing propellers, sirenians are amazingly graceful and fluent when they are in deep water and swimming in groups. Though they are usually placid when alone, in groups they interact in what appear to be play activities—diving or tumbling over in somersaults. "On numerous occasions I've watched them [manatees] frolic with seemingly wild abandon, at times bolting and turning, grasping each other with pectoral fins, leaping partly out of the water, touching flukes and even kissing muzzle to muzzle,"[13] says writer Tim Dietz.

Sirenians at play

Sirenians also play games of chase, follow the leader, or engage in bodysurfing among the waves created by the turbulent water runoffs from electric power plants or in the swift currents formed when the gates of flood dams open. "Sessions of body surfing can last more than an hour, with manatees repeatedly riding the currents in parallel formation," and while engaging in bodysurfing, the manatees "frequently nuzzle one another and vocalize between rides."[14] During these activities, one manatee swims directly behind another, mimicking the first one's every rise for breath, dive, or change of direction.

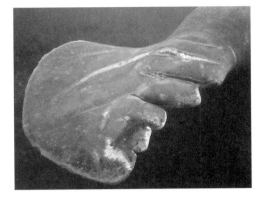

They also interact with humans when they encounter swimmers or divers. Many people have reported manatees swimming between their legs or nuzzling and rubbing against them. Manatees swimming near boat docks often rub themselves against floating logs, the dock itself, or even the boat anchor line, even when humans are close by. This fearlessness around humans puts them in danger of

Grave injuries such as this occur when manatees and power-boats meet (above). A manatee demonstrates playfulness by tugging on an anchor line (below).

being fed the wrong foods, becoming too dependent and accepting of humans, and, of course, of being struck by boats. Florida manatees are most at risk during summer months.

Seasonal migration

Unlike other sea mammals, manatees are unable to regulate their own body temperatures, and though they do have a layer of blubber just under the skin, it is not thick enough to insulate them from cold water. If they are exposed to water below sixty-eight degrees, they are likely to sicken and die. During winter months manatees remain in southern Florida, where the water remains warm all year, or seek shelter in certain lakes and rivers in northern and central Florida, where natural hot springs beneath the ground keep the water temperature a constant seventy-two degrees. Another place manatees are found in the winter is the warm water outflows from electric power plants. Manatees have found these warm water refuges and return year after year.

 Favorite Foods of Sirenians

Other than sea grasses, favorite foods for sirenians are hydrilla, sea lettuce, and water hyacinth. Sirenians are classified as herbivores, but marine biologists have noted that when snails and other invertebrates are attached to the vegetation on which manatees feed, these lower life forms are ingested. Manatees do not regularly consume such animal protein. Dugongs, however, have been reported to occasionally raid fishing nets and eat some of the fish. There have also been reports of Antillean manatees raiding fishing nets, but these same reports say the manatees eat only dead fish, never live ones.

Sirenians in captivity develop tastes for other foods since sea grasses and other natural foods are not easily obtained for them in the quantities they need. Captive manatees are fed a variety of greens such as lettuce and cabbage as well as other fruits and vegetables. Some are occasionally fed dead fish.

In summer, though, Florida manatees expand their search for food farther north. Manatees from Florida have been documented as covering great distances on their seasonal migrations. Some quite commonly travel six hundred to seven hundred miles between their summer and winter homes. Jim Reid, a biologist with the Sirenia Project, a program administered by the Florida Caribbean Science Center and the Biological Resources Division of the U.S. Geological Survey, U.S. Department of the Interior, and based at the University of Florida at Gainesville, said, "Some manatees travel between central Florida and southern Georgia several times in one season."[15]

Chessie—the long-distance traveler

Though most Florida manatees never venture farther than North Carolina, some do travel extensively. One manatee, dubbed Chessie by the media, was particularly adventuresome. This 1,250-pound adult male was first observed in Chesapeake Bay off the coast of Maryland in the summer of 1994. He was still there in October, when the water temperature in the area was dropping rapidly. Fearing he might succumb to cold stress, marine biologists captured him and transported him to a manatee refuge in central Florida. On October 7, before he was released, he was equipped with a satellite-monitored radio tag tied around his tail. For about one week, he remained close to where he was released, then traveled a short distance south to another refuge. Then, for several weeks, there was no sign of the traveling manatee. But Chessie's long-distance forays were far from over.

On January 12, 1995, Jim Reid sighted Chessie hundreds of miles farther south at the outflow of a power plant in Fort Lauderdale. In early February he swam north to the Banana River, where he remained with other manatees until late April. His next trek was to the St. John's River near the Florida-Georgia border, where he took another long break.

On the road again

On June 13 Chessie headed north again. Scientists tracked his progress. On June 15 he was near Brunswick,

Are Manatees Intelligent?

Most people think manatees are less intelligent, and therefore, less interesting than whales or dolphins. Those who work with manatees say this is not so. Dr. Gregory Bossart, chief veterinarian at Miami Seaquarium and professor at the University of Miami, says that the fact that sirenians are not born with many instincts, and that they have relatively long childhoods during which they learn from their mothers, is one indicator of intelligence.

Another indicator of intelligence is that each manatee has its own personality. Most are curious and will boldly examine boat lines, floating logs, dock pilings, and other objects they come across in the water. Georgia and Clover, two manatees rescued as orphaned young calves, were brought to Florida's Blue Springs State Park to begin their reintroduction to the wild after spending their infancies at Sea World in Orlando. Park ranger Wayne Hartley said he could easily tell the two apart. "Georgia was always curious, friendly, and readily approached people. Clover, on the other hand, was always shy and quiet and stayed away from people." A few days after Georgia and Clover were set free, Hartley received calls reporting a manatee swimming behind the sea wall in back of a house or a manatee "stuck" under a local resident's boat dock. The reports were about Georgia, who apparently was seeking out human companionship. No reports were ever turned in about Clover. The following winter, both manatees returned to Blue Springs. Once again, Clover kept to herself while Georgia sought out human contact, even going as far as climbing up onto the shore when people were around.

Georgia; June 17, near Savannah; June 22, Charleston, South Carolina; June 30, Pamlico Sound, North Carolina. During the month of July, he again enjoyed swimming in Chesapeake Bay in Maryland. But he continued northward, surfacing in New Haven, Connecticut, on August 12. Chessie's epic journey took him nineteen days, swimming twenty-five to thirty miles a day, and covering more than fifteen hundred miles.

Once he reached the northernmost point of his remarkable expedition, he reversed direction and followed the same route back to Florida for the winter. Chessie's exploits were followed in newspapers around the country, making him a national celebrity. The following spring people waited to see if Chessie would repeat his adventure. He did start out in the spring and reached North Carolina when his transmitter stopped sending signals. Chessie was last sighted in Norfolk, Virginia, in 1996. It is presumed that shortly after that, he lost his radio tag, but is still making his annual trek. Dr. Lynn Lefebvre, Sirenia Project leader, said, "Individuals, typically males, of many mammalian species may wander beyond the limits of their normal range. Chessie's movements, however, far exceed the normal range of the manatee."[16]

Except in refuges (pictured) and during times of mating, manatees seldom gather together.

The fact that Chessie traveled alone with no other manatee companions was not unusual. Male manatees customarily travel alone. Females travel with only their calves for company. The only time they come together and form groups is at warm water refuges and during mating season. The groups are not permanent and consist of all ages and both sexes. There is no dominant leader and no fighting for position or territory.

Because the feeding grounds and migration patterns of sirenians are predictable and because they are not aggressive and have no way of defending themselves, sirenians have always been easy prey for hunters.

3

Sirenia—Prey
of Humans

SIRENIANS HAVE BEEN hunted by people since the dawn of human history. The first hunters probably attacked them with crude wooden spears in the shallow water where the animals fed. In time, hunters pursued their prey into deeper water with the use of dugout canoes or rafts. Archaeological evidence found in Florida suggests that manatees have been hunted since the Paleo-Indian period (8500–6000 B.C.), the time of the earliest known occupation of this area by humans. This proof comes in the form of fossil manatee bones and ceremonial pipes carved in the shape of manatees buried in prehistoric middens, which are mounds or hills containing ancient refuse left by early civilizations. If manatees were hunted this early, the same is likely to be true for dugongs.

A manatee or dugong was a good catch. Not only did it supply the entire tribe with large quantities of food, but the tough hides proved useful as well, as was discovered by Father Gaspar de Carvajal in the sixteenth century in South America. He wrote, "[The local people] were covered from head to feet with little shields made out of the skins of manatees and these were such that a crossbow would not pierce them." [17] The hides also made durable coverings for canoes and the heavy, dense bones made excellent clubs or mallets.

On the road to danger

Although manatees and dugongs were hunted by tribal societies for thousands of years, only small numbers of animals were taken at any one time, leaving most of the sirenian population free to breed and reproduce. It wasn't until the seventeenth century, when European explorers of the Americas and the Pacific Islands were introduced to these animals, that this pattern changed. Sir Walter Raleigh, on an expedition to Central America in 1596 described manatee meat as "wholesome" and "of good flavor." He also said that because the animal lived in the water it could be considered as fish and therefore could be eaten by Catholics during Lent and on Fridays when meat was forbidden. Since nearly all the explorers were Catholic, classifying manatees as fish encouraged ship captains to hunt the animals as food for their crews.

Monsieur Pomet, chief druggist to King Louis XIV of France wrote, "the Flesh tastes like Veal, but it is a great deal finer, and cover'd in several Parts, with three or four Fingers of thick Fat, of which they make Lard, as they do of Hog's." [18] The ear bones, he said, resembled ivory but were harder. The bones were often ground into powder and either drunk as tea or rubbed on the body to help cure stomach pains, heartburn, and colic. Europeans also used the bones as a substitute for ivory and carved them into ornamental pistol grips and decorative items.

Manatee meat as a commodity

Manatee meat preserved in its own oil remains fresh for up to a year. In a time with no refrigeration, this made manatee meat even more desirable. Manatees soon became a valuable commodity, and hunting expeditions were commissioned by trading companies.

A Dutch company in 1643 commissioned an expedition to Guayana, in South America, to capture and preserve manatee meat to ship to the Caribbean to sell as food for slaves. By 1660 a fleet of twenty Dutch ships a year were taking manatees from Brazil.

By the late 1700s, manatees were captured in such numbers that they were held in pens until they could be harvested for food, oil, and leather. The Pesqueiro Real de Villa Franca (Royal Fishery of France) in Brazil produced

Dugong Hide Mentioned in Records from Biblical Times

Although people living along the coast of the Red Sea have used dugong hide for the soles of their sandals since prehistoric times, some biblical scholars believe that the ancient Israelites also used it as wrapping for the Ark of the Covenant, to protect the sacred object in the hot, sandy desert environment. And inscriptions from biblical times describe palaces of kings as large tentlike structures made from dugong hides. In both cases, it is likely that this material was chosen for its durability and toughness. From a twentieth-century perspective, it is shocking to learn of the slaughter of dozens, perhaps hundreds, of dugongs for construction purposes. In those days, however, the depletion of a rare animal species in the service of royalty was viewed as acceptable.

128,000 pounds of manatee meat and 106,000 pounds of lard harvested from approximately fifteen hundred manatees in just two years.

In Florida, evidence of how rapidly the manatee population was declining is shown by a letter written in 1879. "Then it will surely happen that the peace-loving manatee will be driven away and . . . become but a legend or old man's tale." [19] The writer said it had been eight years since he had seen a manatee, but that when he had come to the area fifteen years earlier, they had been plentiful.

And in 1885, another local observer wrote, "Ten years ago the meat could be bought for 50 cents a pound. Of course the animals are becoming far too scarce to admit of its being sold at all. There is no doubt the manatee is fast becoming an extinct animal . . . the sea cow will pass out of existence." [20]

Dugong oil lit the lamps of Europe

On the other side of the world, explorers probing the coastlines of Australia and the Pacific Islands hunted dugongs that swam in huge herds. Vast numbers of them were taken solely for their oil, which was shipped back to England. In an article written for *Oceans* magazine in 1982, Ben Cropp, an Australian writer and photographer, mentions a book written in 1893, telling of a herd of dugong in Moreton Bay off Brisbane that extended over three miles long by three hundred yards wide. Such a herd would number many thousands. "Today, that same herd still exists," said Cropp, "I have seen them there—but only a dozen or so [dugong]."[21]

Western Europeans were not the only ones exploring the Atlantic and southern Pacific during the seventeenth and eighteenth centuries—and hunting sirenians.

Steller's sea cow story—a lesson for today

In 1741, Vitus Jonassen Bering, a Danish explorer, headed a Russian expedition to the extreme northern Pacific Ocean to measure the distance between Siberia and America. One member of the group was Georg Wilhelm Steller, a German naturalist, who was to record any new plant or animal life they discovered along the way.

In November, the ship ran aground on the shore of an uninhabited island, later to be named Bering Island and the water surrounding it, the Bering Straits. Over the next few months, Bering and several of his crew fell victim to

This Australian Aboriginal painting depicts a small group of dugongs swimming together.

scurvy or to the extreme cold and died. Scurvy is a disease resulting from the lack of vitamin C and was common to sailors of that day. Those who survived the winter salvaged what they could from their wrecked ship and lived on sea otters and another unknown large sea animal that swam near the area.

Steller, meanwhile, made meticulous notes in his journal on this strange beast, which he identified as a member of the "sea cow" family. Steller was correct. The animal was a member of the sirenian family—the only one adapted to cold water. Steller described his sea cow as weighing up to eight thousand pounds. He said it resembled a seal in front, had a head like a buffalo, a skull like a horse, a back like an ox, with round flanks and a belly. The skin was "more like the bark of an oak than the skin of an animal, black, rough, wrinkled, like stone, hard, tough, and hairless which one can hardly do anything to even with an axe or hook."[22] Its lips were covered with thick bristles, and it had tiny, small

Survivors of Bering's 1741 expedition fed on large sea animals that were later named Steller's sea cows, after the naturalist who discovered them.

ear openings and hard horny plates instead of teeth. It did not, however, have nails at the ends of its flippers, nor did it dive.

Steller reported that the meat was delicious and tasted like beef and that the oil smelled and tasted like almonds. He said the beasts, which fed on the kelp that grew on rocks not far from shore, were easy prey for the men who simply waded to them and speared their catch. "These animals are found at all seasons of the year everywhere around the island in great numbers," wrote Steller, "so that the whole population of the eastern coast of Kamchatka [will] always be able to keep itself more than abundantly supplied from them with meat and fat."[23]

By the following summer, having built a small boat from the wreckage of their ship, the crew returned to Russia with furs from seals and sea otters, and tales of the large sea cows so easy to capture and so good to eat.

Steller's sea cow as food for fur traders

Since fur hunting was one of the mainstays of the Russian economy, Bering Island and nearby Copper Island became regular stops for future expeditions. In 1887, naturalist Leonard Stejneger wrote that from 1743 to 1763, "Hardly a winter passed without one or more parties spending eight or nine months in hunting fur-animals there, during which time the crews lived almost exclusively on the meat of the sea-cow."[24]

Methods used to hunt these northern sea cows were extremely wasteful. Animals were speared in shallow water, but because of their huge size, they were not brought immediately to the shore. Instead, they were simply left to die, and people used only those that washed ashore while their carcasses were still fresh. Then, many hunters took only what they considered the choicest bits of meat, leaving the rest of the body to rot where it lay. The carcasses of animals that had been fatally wounded, but not butchered, were allowed to drift out to sea.

A Russian mining engineer, on assignment on Copper Island in 1754, reported that there were no more sea cows in that area. He and his crew, therefore, camped on Bering Island where the sea cows were still in good supply. Observing the thoughtless methods of the hunters, he predicted that soon there would be no more sea cows at all. He petitioned the authorities to regulate the hunting of the sea cows, but the petition was ignored. Thirteen years later his prediction came true. There were no more sea cows.

The extinction of this animal, later named Steller's sea cow (*Hydrodamalis gigas*), took just twenty-seven years. Today, all that is known of it are the notes left by Steller, bones that were left on Bering Island, and fossil records of bones found along the Alaskan and California coasts. Ancestors of Steller's sea cow ranged over much of the Pacific Ocean 5 million years ago and they swam as far south as central California around twenty thousand years ago. By the time Bering's crew found them in 1741, scientists think the population had been reduced to only around two thousand animals.

The thoughtlessness and greed that led to the sea cow's demise stands as a stark example of how quickly a species can be exterminated. But because Steller's sea cow inhabited a remote region of the world, little attention was paid

Due to overly aggressive hunting, the Steller's sea cow was extinct only twenty-seven years after its discovery.

to its extinction. Commercial hunting of other sirenians continued well into the twentieth century, especially in Central and South America.

The hunting of manatees

Commercial hunting of sirenians has been outlawed internationally since 1973, when they were declared endangered under the U.S. Endangered Species Act. Before that time, from the mid-1800s to the 1930s, the major product produced from manatees was *mixira,* the meat fried in its own oil. In Brazil, between 1935 and 1954, thousands of skins were exported to be made into machinery belts, gaskets, hoses, and other items. And even in Florida where manatee hunting had been outlawed since 1907, "manatees were eaten at times during the depression of the 1930s and during World War II when other meat was scarce."[25] There are no statistics on the history of dugong hunting, but hundreds of thousands of them were undoubtedly taken.

There is a vast difference between commercial hunting where thousands of animals are taken to sell for profit and the traditional subsistence hunting engaged in by aboriginal tribes where only those animals which can be utilized for food or religious purposes are taken. Dugongs are still hunted because they are an integral part of the religion and culture of certain aboriginal tribes of Australia and the Torres Straits. And while all hunting of manatees is officially outlawed in the Americas, some tribal hunting continues in certain areas of Central and South America. Nearly all tribal hunting is done with age-old traditional methods.

Hunting such a huge animal with a harpoon from a canoe is dangerous. Many hunters have been caught in their own ropes and towed out to sea, or rendered unconscious with a blow from the animal's powerful tail. Other hunters drown when they are caught in unexpected storms. Among peoples where sirenian hunting is part of the culture, there is deep respect for both the animal and the hunter. A code of strict ethics and complex traditions govern everything concerned with the hunt, from the preparation to the dividing up of the meat. A tribe may have only one official dugong

Superstitions and Beliefs

Many superstitions and beliefs have evolved concerning sirenians. Fishermen in Cameroon, in western Africa, believed manatees lived in caves in the river and could drown people. The Kalabrai tribe of western Africa regarded the manatee as sacred or as a reincarnated human being. If a manatee was killed, the hunter had to remain in his house for three days and apply special substances to himself while the women of his family sang at dawn and dusk in hopes of appeasing the animal's wounded spirit. After this ritual, a piece of manatee meat was given to the head of each household in the village so that he could lay it before the shrine of his forefathers.

As late as the 1960s, the Rama Indians of Nicaragua bathed in manatee blood after a hunt, perhaps to imbue the hunter with the strength of his prey. Later, the hunter would return the bones to the place where he killed the animal, believing this would draw more manatees to the area, presumably to ensure further hunting opportunities.

or manatee hunter at a time, and only he is allowed to stalk and kill the animal. Before becoming a dugong or manatee hunter, there are many years of apprenticeship and a rigorous initiation.

Traditional hunting methods

Tribal methods of hunting sirenians, though they differ in some aspects, are remarkably similar in widely separated parts of the world and have changed little over the centuries. The following description, written by William Dampier, an English sailor plying the coasts of Nicaragua and Honduras in 1681, provides a vivid picture of a typical manatee hunt conducted by the Mosquito Indians of that area.

> One of the Mosquitos . . . sits in the stern, the other kneels down in the head, and both paddle till they come to a place where they expect their game. Then they lye still or paddle very softly, looking well about them; and he that is in the head of the Canoa lays down his paddle, and stands up with his striking staff in his hand. The . . . end of the line is made fast to the Harpoon, which is at the great end of the staff. . . . When he strikes, the Harpoon presently comes out of the staff, and as the manatee swims away, the line runs off from

the bob. . . . When the manatee begins to be tired, it lyeth still, and the [Mosquito] men . . . begin to hale in the line. When the manatee feels them he swims away again, with the Canoa after him. . . . Thus the Canoa is towed with violent motion, till the manatees strength decays. . . . At length when the Creature's strength is spent, they hale up to the Canoa's side, and knock it on the head, and tow it to the nearest shore where they make it fast.[26]

Twentieth-century tribal hunting methods

Modern technology has modified tribal hunting somewhat. In 1982, Ben Cropp met with members of the Bardi, a tribe of aboriginal people who, after many generations of living in city slums and being snubbed by Australians of European descent, decided to return to their original homelands and their traditional way of life. Cropp was offered the rare opportunity to go along on a dugong hunt.

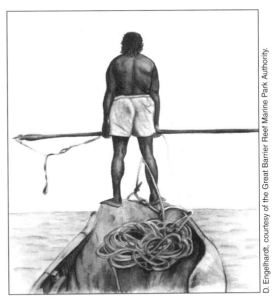

Armed with a harpoon, a Mosquito Indian searches for his prey during a manatee hunt.

D. Engelhardt, courtesy of the Great Barrier Reef Marine Park Authority.

Cropp and two Bardi, the hunter and the boat driver, rode to the hunting grounds in a motor-powered dinghy. But when they approached the dugong area, the boatman removed the motor and replaced it with a sculling oar wrapped in a bag to muffle its sound. "This is dugong country. Now we go real quietly, do not even cough," said the Bardi hunter, cocking a worried eye at the faint lapping of the fuel in the half-empty tank.

As the dinghy drifted along the edge of the dugong feeding grounds, two dugongs poked their heads above the water. The boatman slowly sculled the dinghy closer, saying he wanted the dugongs to get used to his boat. There were more than a dozen animals around the boat, but Cropp's guide was going after the first two. For about an hour, they watched the two dugongs as they popped up to breathe, then submerge again. Finally, the hunter said, "We go in next time." He stood on the bow, his harpoon at the ready.

When the dugongs surfaced again, the hunter paddled closer. One dugong dove deep, but the other remained near the surface. The hunter hurled his harpoon. It found its mark and sank into the flesh. The force of thrust pulled the man into the air. He remained suspended for a few seconds, then toppled into the water with a great splash. He sank below the water, then surfaced, and his partner reached for him and pulled him back into the dinghy.

At that moment, a sudden snap tightened the rope. The dinghy was being towed swiftly through the water faster than when they had been using the motor. The great animal surfaced ahead. The two hunters pulled the rope, trying to bring the dugong closer. "I knew how the old whalers felt when they hung on to a sounding leviathan," Cropp said.

The dugong showed no signs of tiring and continued to swim powerfully, trailing the boat behind him. One of the hunters dived over the side and looped a heavy rope around the dugong's tail. "We've got him now!" he shouted.

Both hunters held the tail, twisting it so the dugong could not raise his head and breathe. The dugong expelled

A Bardi tribesman drives his harpoon into the back of a surfaced dugong.

his final breath and drowned. They rode back to their starting point where they were greeted by the entire village. The men helped lug the huge carcass onto the beach and the animal was butchered, cooked, and shared by all. Cropp said, "I have to admit it tasted good."[27]

Limits on tribal hunting

Although several tribes are allowed to hunt dugongs, efforts are being made to control the numbers of animals they take. Many tribes are working with the government to accomplish this. For example, more than 90 percent of the tribes near Brisbane, Australia, who have traditionally hunted dugongs agreed to stop taking them in Queensland waters. Others agree to take only a certain number of animals a year.

Opponents of aboriginal hunting say that because the tribes are using twentieth-century aluminum boats with motors instead of dugout canoes, and monofilament line and steel harpoon heads instead of more primitive ones, they continue to be a threat to the dugong population. But Cropp disagrees. He points out that aboriginal hunting has built-in protections for the dugong, since cultural traditions dictate the number and qualifications of hunters and control the distribution of the meat. He also disputes the idea that the introduction of modern technology has increased the numbers of dugong caught, pointing out that outboard motors are mostly used only to bring the hunters to and from the hunting areas, that their motors are frequently not working, and that once in the hunting grounds, only traditional methods are used.

But not every aboriginal sirenian hunter follows traditional practices, and some hunting of both dugongs and manatees still occurs for noncultural reasons.

Current status of sirenians and hunting

Aside from tribal and traditional hunting, sirenians are still hunted in several countries today despite protective laws. This is often the case in developing and poor countries where civil unrest, war, poverty, and other human problems place sirenian protection at low priority. The West African

Instead of primitive harpoon heads like this one, most aboriginal tribespeople now use steel versions that are more of a threat to dugongs.

manatee has already been hunted almost to extinction as has the Antillean manatee in several places. Farmers in Guinea-Bissau, in western Africa, kill manatees to sell their meat and to prevent their eating the rice that is cultivated in the rivers.

In several countries in Central America, manatee meat is sold quite openly despite laws that make such sales illegal. In the Dominican Republic and Mexico, carved manatee bones are sold as ornaments and ground-up bones are sold for medicine.

In India, some Muslims kill dugongs because they resemble pigs, which Muslims consider undesirable animals, and some Hindu fishermen kill them because they fear that they will tear nets and eat their fish.

SireNews, a newsletter for an international organization devoted to saving sirenians, reported that in 1997, Wil Mahei, a field specialist in manatee conservation in Belize, found several incidents of recently slaughtered manatees with the prime areas of meat stripped away. "I am in the field almost every day and have never seen or heard of manatee meat for sale in Belize; but I have had people confirm to me that they have bought the meat in Guatemala,"[28] Mahei said.

The same issue of *SireNews* reported that in February 1997, sixteen Bogotá, Colombia, fishermen corralled and killed four manatees, including a cow and calf, to obtain two tons of meat. *SireNews* staff said this was one of the worst ecological tragedies of recent times in that country. This story pointed out that in the Magdelena River of Colombia, where at one time manatees flourished, at the last count there were only thirty-five left.

Incidental hunting

Just as some commercial hunting of sirenians continues in spite of laws against it, so does some subsistence hunting occur outside of those places where it is allowed. But there is yet another kind of hunting that threatens sirenians—incidental hunting, in which the dugong or manatee is not the main target of the hunt, but is caught in nets, traps, or other means of capturing other prey. The profit realized from these accidentally taken sirenians is great enough that some fishermen have begun to intentionally trap the sea mammals.

 ## Medicinal Value of Sirenian Bones

Many cultures firmly believe that ground sirenian bones, sirenian body fat, and dugong tears hold curative and/or magical powers. Today, as in the past, in many places in Australia, certain Pacific Islands, and remote areas of Central and South America, manatee or dugong bones are ground up and used to treat kidney problems, colic, dysentery, urinary problems, and even to relieve labor pains during childbirth. The inner ear bones, believed particularly valuable, are sometimes kept as charms against bad luck or witchcraft as well. The Comoro Islanders give the powdered bones to people with ulcers. And in Malaysia, the dugong's abundant tears are collected and used as an aphrodisiac.

And it is not only the animal's bones that are used for medicinal purposes: Meat from the head is used to cure headaches and earaches, and body fat and fat from the animal's intestines are believed by some people to be able to prevent or cure illness.

Dugong oil, which is similar to cod liver oil, is used for many purposes and, according to the beliefs of several aboriginal peoples of Australia, also possesses strong medicinal value. The fishermen of Sri Lanka use dugong oil as a cure for dysentery. The Moharrais of Madagascar rub their bodies with dugong blubber or body fat to treat skin diseases, even conditions as serious as leprosy.

No part of the animal is wasted. Even the dung is considered valuable as a medicine or as a good luck charm, and, in the past, was often rubbed on a dugong or manatee hunter's body for good luck.

Helene Marsh, a prominent dugong researcher in Australia, along with others involved in dugong protection, has called for increasing the numbers of Dugong Protection Areas along the Great Barrier Reef. In addition, Marsh has requested a ban on mesh netting in these areas.

Incidental hunting also occurs regularly in western Africa as well as in Central and South America. Fishermen who take sirenians illegally do not realize how much harm they are doing themselves. Because sirenians eat so many of the plants that grow in the water, they help to preserve the natural ecology. When the manatees are gone, there will be an excess of floating plants, which will eventually impede the passage of light. This absence of light will kill the microscopic algae that produce oxygen, which, in turn, will reduce the amount of fish in those areas.

Captured for its meat and hide, a dugong hangs in an Australian Aboriginal net.

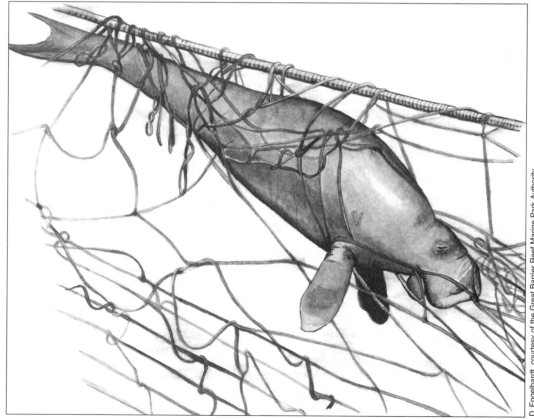

D. Engelhardt, courtesy of the Great Barrier Reef Marine Park Authority.

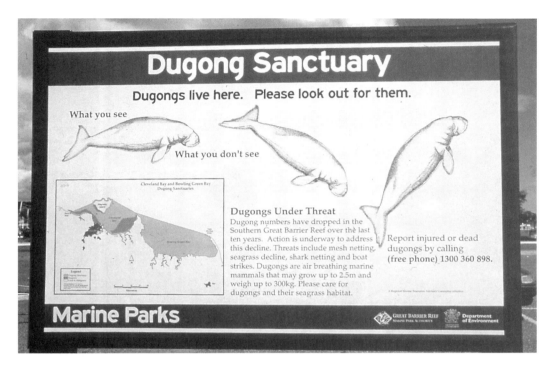

A small group of eighteenth-century Russians brought about the extinction of a species, Steller's sea cow, by killing two thousand of them. Today there are far more than two thousand sirenians in the world, but many individual populations of both manatees and dugongs number fewer than that. Without awareness of just how precarious sirenian populations are, future generations may have only fossils and old records that tell about dugongs and manatees. Sirenians are threatened by more than hunting. Perhaps the largest threat to sirenians today is the development of coastal areas for human use.

Sanctuaries such as this one have been established along Australia's Great Barrier Reef.

4

Human Encroachments into Sirenian Environments

APPROXIMATELY ONE THOUSAND people a day move to Florida. From 1970 to 1996, the number of full-time residents in the state nearly doubled. In addition to full-time residents, latest estimates show over 770,000 part-time residents who spend the winter in Florida. And in addition to full- and part-time residents, Florida hosts over 42 million visitors each year. Why do so many people flock to Florida? They come because of the subtropical climate and hundreds of miles of inviting coastline and inland waterways. These are the same waters used by manatees.

As more people take up residence along Florida's coastlines, the need arises for more housing, expanded roadways, facilities for water and sewage treatment, schools, shopping and entertainment centers, and other services. The rapid growth of the human population along Florida's coasts has resulted in the development of large amounts of coastal lands for residential, industrial, and commercial purposes. It has meant dredging canals and locks for more boat traffic and for marinas. These activities directly invade manatee habitats.

Loss of habitat through overdevelopment of coastal areas

Wastewater and sewage runoff from homes and businesses drain into the waterways; chemicals from lawn fertilizers and insect-control programs seep into the water from under the ground. These pollutants are absorbed by plant growth and then ingested by the sea life that feed on the plants. Studies confirm that there are contaminants and pollutants in manatees' systems. Although at the present time there is no direct evidence that these contaminants are at high enough levels to cause disease, no one knows the effects of these pollutants on future generations of the species.

Dredging the canals does even more harm. The bottom soil is churned up, releasing large amounts of free-floating sediment that blocks the amount of sunlight filtering through the water. Without this sunlight, the sea grasses stop growing. But these grasses form the mainstay of the sirenian diet.

What is true for the Florida manatee is also true for other species of sirenians. Human intrusion into sirenian habitats the world over is occurring at an ever-increasing

The overdevelopment of coastal areas in Florida is responsible for damaging manatee habitat through soil erosion, pollution, wastewater drainage, and increased boat traffic.

rate. In Central and South America, the rain forests are being chopped down to make way for agricultural land to meet the needs of the growing human population. This problem is addressed by Reynolds and Odell, who say,

> The Amazonian manatee could ultimately become extinct, not because of hunting pressure, which the species has faced for millennia, but due to habitat destruction. Elimination of forests causes erosion and increases runoff that can contain pollutants. Deforestation may also lead to large-scale reduction of water levels, which could threaten manatee survival during dry-season fasts. Water and biogeochemical cycles change when the land is denuded of forests, and vegetation available for the manatees will decrease. As with the other sirenians, survival of the Amazonian manatees depends on managing human activities.[29]

Jeremy Tager, coordinator of the North Queensland Conservation Council in Australia, says the future of the dugong faces the same types of problems—overdevelopment of coastal areas and the subsequent effects on coastal ecosystems and sea grasses. In fact, dugongs are threatened throughout their wide habitat. As is pointed out by the authors of *The Sierra Club Handbook on Seals and Sirenians*, "The deterioration of habitat throughout the Arabian

Dredging canals stirs up sediment which blocks the sunlight needed by the manatee's main sources of food: sea grasses and other marine plants.

Gulf, due to oil pollution, land reclamation, and military activities, threatens the dugongs' existence there."[30]

The danger to sirenians comes not only from developing coastal areas for human use, but from direct encroachment of sirenian habitat in the waterways themselves.

Speeding boats ruin sea grass

One of the major dangers to Florida manatees is the high number of commercial and pleasure watercraft using the waterways. In 1997, there were 794,996 boats registered to Florida residents; 33,650 of these were commercial fishing or tugboats and 761,346 were pleasure craft. In addition to residents using Florida's waterways, thousands of tourists either tow their boats or visit on their boats.

Each year several manatees are killed in Florida as a result of collisions with boats. Almost every manatee in Florida has, at one time or other, been hit by a boat propeller. Although most manatees do recover from propeller cuts, not all do, and the scars remain throughout the manatee's life.

According to the U.S. Fish and Wildlife Service's Florida Manatee Recovery Plan of 1996, "The major threats to Florida manatees are collisions with watercraft, which account for about 25 percent of known manatee deaths in Florida annually, and the destruction and degradation of habitat caused by widespread development throughout much of the species' Florida range."[31]

Bonnie Bilyeu Gordon described a visit she made to the Miami Seaquarium treatment center with Gregory Bossart, the Seaquarium's chief veterinarian, where he was treating a manatee injured by a boat propeller. "Dr. Bossart's beast had big, open gashes. The gashes had allowed in other infections, and the manatee was also suffering from pneumonia."[32]

No less dangerous to manatees than propellers are speeding boats. "A boat moving at thirty-five miles per hour can knock out a manatee that's surfacing for air. It will just sink to the bottom and drown,"[33] says Judith Vallee, president of the Save the Manatee Club. Aside from the direct

Speeding boats endanger manatees by colliding with them and silting up the waters in which the animals' food grows.

danger to manatees themselves, fast-moving boats churn up the water. As in dredging, this violent water action lifts bottom sediment, cutting down the amount of sunlight that reaches the sea grasses.

Although most of the statistics about boating accidents and sirenians pertain to the United States, as pleasure boating increases in other countries, so will the dangers to sirenians in those countries. But boating isn't the only human activity putting sirenians at peril.

Floodgates and canal locks that control the water flow present another danger to manatees. When gates are left partially open, manatees sometimes swim through them. They become trapped in the water current from upstream and drown. Remote-controlled gates sometimes crush manatees as they come down.

Fishermen and sirenians

While pleasure boats present the greatest dangers to sirenians in the United States, in other countries manatees and dugongs become trapped in nets used by private and commercial fishermen. Though gill nets are not often used in Florida waters, they are the predominant method of catching fish in the waters of the Pacific and Indian Oceans. Gill nets can kill dugongs, turtles, and whales. "They become tangled, and they drown in 4 to 8 minutes," said Jeremy Tager. "Gill netting is the primary cause of dugong mortality."[34] Fishing nets not only harm dugongs, but their food sources. Fishing nets are used where fish gather, and fish gather in and among sea grasses. As the nets drag through the sea grass beds, the grasses are uprooted and destroyed.

Again, like boaters, most fishermen behave responsibly and try to avoid catching dugongs, or if they do catch them, they release them quickly. According to a 1997 story in a Sydney, Australia, newspaper, however, "Some dugongs caught in nets are being decapitated and disembowelled by fishers trying to avoid detection."[35] This type of activity was also reported in another newspaper, "Conservationists

Manatee Deaths in Florida, 1974–1997

Cause of Death	24-Year Totals 1974–1997	10-Year Average 1986–1995	5-Year Average 1991–1995	1996 Total Deaths	1997 Total Deaths
Watercraft-Related	763 (23%)	43 (27%)	43 (25%)	60 (14%)	55 (23%)
Floodgates/Canal Locks	136 (4%)	6 (4%)	9 (5%)	10 (2%)	8 (3%)
Other Human-Related	86 (3%)	4 (2%)	6 (3%)	0	8 (3%)
Infant	688 (21%)	41 (25%)	48 (27%)	61 (15%)	61 (25%)
Other Natural Causes	563 (17%)	28 (17%)	26 (15%)	118 (28%)	47 (20%)
Undetermined	1,033 (32%)	39 (24%)	43 (25%)	166 (40%)	63 (26%)
Total Deaths	3,269	161 average	175 average	415	242

Source: Florida Department of Environmental Protection, *Manatee News Quarterly,* October–December 1997.

accuse fishermen of slashing open the bodies of drowned dugongs so they sink, in an attempt to hide the evidence."[36]

Dugongs at special risk

Although the selling of dugong meat is outlawed in most places today, some eager buyers remain. Because of this, there are also increasing incidences of fishermen not only keeping the dugongs they capture accidentally, but actually trying to capture them intentionally to sell the meat.

Even when fishermen find and release dugongs from nets, the animals are still at great risk. Dugongs appear to be extremely sensitive animals and, as reported in *The Sierra Club Handbook on Seals and Sirenians,* "Dugongs may be susceptible to capture stress, which means that even the animals that escape from nets [or are released from them] or hunters may later die."[37]

"I've lived in this ecosystem for years, but then, I like danger."

And writer Peter Spielmann reports, "Dr. A. Smith of Australia's federal science agency, the Commonwealth Scientific and Industrial Research Organization, has forecast that the killing of as few as 15 dugongs a year in the southern reef area could put that population on the decline to oblivion." [38]

But not everyone agrees that fishing is doing serious harm to dugongs. Ted Loveday, president of a group of two hundred to three hundred fishermen in Australia, feels that dugongs are "not critically endangered and are not at risk of extinction." [39] He blames the decline of dugongs on real estate developers taking large segments of the Queensland coastline.

Fishing nets are not the only nets that endanger dugongs, nor the only kind of nets that spark controversy over their use. In Australia and other countries, nets are customarily strung along beach areas to keep sharks away from swimmers. The nets do protect the swimmers from sharks, but they also sometimes trap dugongs, causing them to drown.

War is another human activity that threatens sirenians. In the short but bloody Persian Gulf War of 1991, many dugongs were killed in bombings. Additional numbers died then and later when they collided with mines. Overdevelopment of shore areas, boating, fishing, and war are human activities that are dangerous to sirenians. Many humans do not consider the needs of these sea mammals. But what about activities that bring humans into direct contact with the animals—not to harm them, but to study or admire them?

Too much human contact?

Swimming or skin diving with manatees has become a popular leisure activity in Florida. People come from Asia, Europe, and all over North America to swim with them. Posted guidelines and rules remind divers not to pursue, ride, poke, or harass the animals. If a manatee approaches a human, the human may extend one hand only to touch the animal. Touching with both hands is considered "riding," and is against the law. Sometimes, visitors find these rules difficult to follow. Manatees are friendly and curious. Swimmers and divers report many incidents of the animal nuzzling between their legs or just waiting to be petted. Many of them roll over, inviting a belly scratch. In some ways this is good. People who swim with the manatees fall in love with them and are more likely to support programs to safeguard the animals and their habitat. Cameron Shaw, recently of the wildlife refuge at Crystal River in Florida, says, "We've found that swimming with manatees fosters a great advocacy for the species as well as for the whole ecosystem."[40]

Jim Reid, a biologist working with the Sirenia Project, also feels the swim programs are not harmful. He feels most people abide by the rules, that the river remains a safe place for manatees, and that petting does not hurt them. "There are very few manatee carcasses recovered from that [Crystal River] region."[41]

But some people who work with manatees are concerned about people and manatees interacting. In May 1996, members of the Marine Mammal Commission (an independent congressional advisory agency based in Bethesda, Maryland) sent a letter to the U.S. Fish and Wildlife Service urging them to try to stop the "blatant harassment of manatees at Three Sisters' Spring [in Florida]."[42] The commission also suggested the use of more field officers to oversee the springs and the establishment of a permit system for the recreational use of waterways frequented by manatees.

Officials and members of Save the Manatee Club, one of the leading organizations involved in promoting manatee awareness and protection, are also concerned that the increasingly large numbers of people diving in the springs will alter the environment and the animals' natural behavior. They encourage people to go to parks or viewing areas to watch manatees, but not to touch or interact with them. Sirenians have to contend with natural hazards as well as those presented by humans.

Natural hazards to sirenians

Although most species of sirenians have no natural enemies, they are occasionally attacked by sharks. And the Amazonian manatee is preyed on by alligators, jaguars,

Sirenia-Friendly Boating, Diving, and Swimming Practices

- If you drive a motorboat, slow to idle or no-wake speed when you see a sign indicating that you are in a manatee area—or if you see a manatee. A swirl of water at the surface sometimes indicates that a manatee is nearby. At other times you may hear the breathing of a manatee or see its back, tail, or snout.
- If you dive and encounter a manatee, do not approach it. Let it approach you. If it doesn't, leave it be. Never touch a manatee unless it touches you first.
- If you water ski or jet ski, always choose areas free of manatees.
- If you fish, never discard monofilament line or other objects into the water.
- If you see an injured or dead manatee, or a tagged manatee, call Florida's Manatee Hotline: 800-DIAL-FMP.

Divers should never approach manatees. Rather, they should let the animals approach them first.

Alligators (pictured) prey on Amazonian manatees.

caimans, and piranha fish. In Florida, once in a while, an alligator will spot a manatee's radio tag antenna and go after it, thinking it is a fishing line and that perhaps there is a fish on the end.

Aside from other animals, severe weather conditions are another danger to sirenians. Monsoons, cyclones, typhoons, hurricanes, or tidal waves can toss the animals out of the water as well as rip up sea grass beds. Periods of extremely heavy rains cause flooding that affects all sea life. In Australia, twenty-seven dugongs were stranded as a result of cyclone Kathy in 1984, and over two hundred dugongs died as a result of heavy flooding that silted the river and killed the sea grasses in 1992. These are just two examples of tragedies that occur with extreme weather.

Floods

In the spring of 1998, extremely wet conditions led to too much water in Lake Okeechobee, in south-central Florida. To save the lake, engineers released the extra water into the canals and waterways that are usually brackish. The water brought with it large amounts of sediment, mud, and microorganisms that lived in the lake. These additions to the canals silted the water, once again causing damage to the sea grasses, which resulted in less food for the manatees. Also, adding so much freshwater at one time to the canals and inlets reduced the natural salinity of that water. Invertebrates such as oysters and clams, and microorganisms that require high salinity either died or fled the areas. However, other forms of sea life, including bacteria and microorganisms new to the area, thrived. Soon fishermen and swimmers were finding sick fish with large open sores. It is believed that the decreased salinity of the water and the unfamiliar microorganisms may have caused the fish to become sick. Other life forms were also affected. A number of swimmers suffered from similar open sores on their legs. While the manatees seemed unaffected by these sores, the long-term effects of ingesting the microorganisms along with other food or of swimming in waters infested with them are not known.

Droughts

Just as flooding causes hazards to sirenians, so do periods of extreme drought. In the Amazon, where there are long dry and wet seasons, many manatees sicken and die during the dry period.

In Florida, where water temperatures in winter can fall well below the 68 degrees Fahrenheit needed by manatees, the animals are at particular peril. Each time there is a severe cold spell in Florida, several manatees are found dead. When necropsies are performed on the recovered carcasses, scientists find that the natural layer of blubber between the body and the skin is gone and that there is no food in the stomach. This indicates the animals, instead of

Although they do not seem to affect manatees at present, changes in water conditions due to flooding and sewage treatment may produce long-term health problems in the mammals.

eating, depleted their own body fat. It is not clear, though, whether the manatees died of starvation or from the effects of thermal stress.

Red tide

In the spring of 1996 over four hundred Florida manatees (nearly 20 percent of the state's population) died of pneumonia. Tests later showed that the cause of the pneumonia and subsequent death was a virulent outbreak of red tide, poisonous algae that sometimes infest the water. Manatees ingest the algae along with their food. Red tide outbreaks occur at irregular and unpredictable intervals. In years that outbreaks are particularly heavy, the water actually turns red.

An outbreak of red tide in 1982 sickened and killed many manatees, but unlike the 1996 outbreak, not all of the affected animals died. In the 1982 outbreak, the animals' brains and central nervous systems were affected instead of their lungs. Other aquatic life is also affected by red tide. Birds who ingest infected shellfish become disoriented and often cannot fly.

Red tide is a poisonous algae that has been responsible for the deaths of hundreds of Florida manatees.

No one knows what causes red tide, or why the manatees, who are usually able to fight off diseases, are so susceptible, but many scientists believe one factor is increased pollution levels in the water. The pollution may affect the manatees' immune systems, making them unable to fight off the poison from the algae.

Other causes of manatee deaths

Manatees sometimes sicken and die from bacterial poisoning, such as salmonella. They get colds and, occasionally, pneumonia. They suffer from blocks in their digestive systems caused by the ingestion of fishing line or hooks, wire, plastic sheeting, and other discarded items.

In 1997, several manatees died from a bacterial infection of the intestines and lungs. They may also be subject to certain viruses which are not yet understood. "It is very likely that viruses that are as yet undescribed in manatees initiated several of these cases [unknown causes of illness and death]. As our ability to isolate and identify viruses improves, fewer cases will have a purely bacterial etiology."[43]

The manatee's ability to recover from serious illnesses and wounds may one day help scientists find a cure for human diseases such as AIDS.

Could manatees help humans stay healthy?

Manatees rarely die from illness because they have an extraordinarily well developed immune system. This highly developed immune system also helps them recover from boat propeller cuts and other wounds. Some scientists would like to study why and how the manatee's immune system works so well and apply this knowledge to helping humans, particularly those who suffer from diseases like AIDS, but so far, no one has been willing to fund such a study.

Threats to sirenians can be divided into two categories: those caused either directly or indirectly by humans and those caused by nature. The big question is what can humans do to lessen the threats.

5

Saving Sirenians

THE FIRST STEP in protecting any species is to gain as much knowledge and understanding about them and their requirements as is possible. Reynolds and Odell say,

> To understand sirenians, one must consider at least three factors: the biology of the species, including habitat, physiology, reproduction and other factors; the place sirenians occupy in certain coastal or riverine ecosystems; and the relationship that the sirenians and their ecosystems have had, and continue to have, with people.[44]

To obtain this information, scientists engage in research. The sirenians are a small order, and the five species have many similarities. Thus, the methods and findings used in the study of the Florida manatee are representative of those used in sirenian research throughout the world.

Researching sirenians

There are two major methods of conducting research on wild animals: observing them in their natural habitat and studying captured animals under controlled conditions. Observing sirenians in their natural habitat enables scientists to gain essential knowledge about the animals' basic needs. Direct observation of manatees and their use of the waterways also allows conservation managers to assess the effects on sirenians and their habitats of such human activities as coastal development, placement and use of navigation channels, and the use of these waterways by small and large boats.

Sea World's manatee facility in Florida is one of the sites involved in sirenian rehabilitation and research.

Captive animals, those that have been rescued and are being cared for at rehabilitation facilities, provide opportunities for scientists to study the animals' biology, physiology, and behavior.

The primary purpose of all sirenian research is to promote conditions so that populations grow to the point where they are no longer endangered or threatened. To accomplish this, protection and conservation programs identify sirenian habitats and then determine the number of animals living in them. Only when basic data have been collated and evaluated can scientists recommend ways of reducing disturbances, injury, and death.

Since the information is gathered by several different agencies and organizations, it is essential to coordinate, monitor, and evaluate programs as they are put in place, and to update them as needed.

Identifying habitats and the number of animals using them

The easiest way to find sirenian habitats and current population trends is to use aerial tracking to survey known or suspected areas of use. Tracking is done from small, high-winged aircraft flying at low altitudes. While aerial tracking can positively identify habitat locations, it can only estimate the number of animals because it is difficult to see

Alphabet Soup: The Many Agencies Involved in the Protection and Saving of Manatees

In Florida, the effort to save and protect manatees is shared among many different federal, state, and local agencies. Knowing each one and its exact responsibilities can be confusing, first because there are so many, and, second, because their responsibilities often overlap.

The U.S. Fish and Wildlife Service (USFWS) is a federal agency charged with the conservation of the nation's wildlife. This agency operates the National Wildlife Refuge (NWR) system. USFWS also enforces the Endangered Species Act (ESA) and the Marine Mammal Protection Act, as they apply to manatees. Through its National Biological Service department, it also sponsors the Sirenia Project, based out of the University of Florida at Gainesville, which conducts field research and tags manatees for aerial, satellite, and visual tracking.

The Army Corps of Engineers (ACOE) is a federal agency that monitors water resources such as rivers, lakes, harbors, and wetlands. ACOE helps to locate and identify all areas used by Florida manatees so it can assess the effects of human activities on those areas.

Florida's Department of Environmental Protection (FDEP) oversees the administration, supervision, development, and conservation of Florida's natural resources. There are many subdivisions of FDEP. The Bureau of Protected Species Management (BPSM) sets boating speed regulations for manatee protection and handles the placement and maintenance of signs posted in manatee areas. The Florida Marine Research Institute (FMRI) conducts research and is responsible for salvaging manatee carcasses. Under FMRI are the Marine Mammal Section (MMS) and the Coastal and Marine Resource Assessment (CAMRA) departments. FDEP also manages water quality programs, wetlands development regulation, pollution control, solid waste and recycling, and location of power plants—all of which affect manatees.

The Florida Marine Patrol (FMP) is the law enforcement agency charged with policing speeding boaters and regulating other water-related activities.

The Florida Game and Freshwater Fish Commission (FGFFC) manages wildlife and freshwater fisheries resources and conducts aerial surveys of manatee areas.

On a more local level, the Department of Community Affairs (DCA) is the state land planning agency of Florida. It monitors plans of local governments as they affect manatee-sensitive areas.

In addition to the federal, state, and local organizations, private agencies such as Save the Manatee Club, a major utility (Florida Power and Light Company), and several aquariums and zoological parks are involved in manatee protection in Florida.

manatees from the air, especially in murky water. Therefore, counts vary from day to day. In the last few years, manatee counts in Florida have risen from approximately twelve hundred in the mid-1980s to over two thousand in 1997. The higher numbers are less likely to indicate greater numbers of animals than better tracking methods. Today, surveys are made throughout the state, whereas they used to be conducted only in selected areas. Thus, more manatees are counted.

Aerial tracking does not provide information on migration routes or the behavior of specific animals. One way to acquire such data is to tag animals that have been rescued and released. VHF (very high frequency) radio or satellite transmitters allow researchers to follow an individual for up to two years. The transmitter, which floats on or just below the surface of the water, is attached to a flexible six-foot tether on a belt that is tied around the base of the animal's tail. For safety purposes, the belt is designed to break free if it does get caught and to fall off automatically after two years. The VHF tags are relatively inexpensive, costing $500 each, but they can only be read by handheld receivers. Satellite transmitters, though, which cost $5,000 each, can be read by researchers via the Internet or computer with satellite hookups. Obviously satellite tags are preferred, but lack of funding limits their use.

VHF transmitters enable scientists to study manatee migratory habits. More expensive satellite transmitters are also employed on a limited basis.

Tagged animals are also stamped with an ID mark by freeze drying (which does not hurt the animal) and equipped with a Passive Integrated Transponder (PIT), a rice-grain-sized pellet that is implanted under the skin and remains with the animal for life. If that animal is ever rescued again, or is found dead, a scanning device reads the PIT tag, providing additional information on the animal's identity and history.

Sight tracking

In addition to radio and satellite tracking, manatees are tracked by sight. The tops of the transmitters are color banded for this purpose, and marine biologists use an extensive photo ID catalog identifying over one thousand manatees by their individual scar patterns. Jim Reid, who works extensively with manatees in Florida, says, "With the photo ID system, we can track individuals by sight and keep track of their migration, behavior, feeding, mating, and birthing patterns, then extrapolate [extend] this to the larger population."[45]

One of the most helpful tools in studying and coordinating the various data collected about sirenians is the geographic information system (GIS), a computer program that can store, integrate, and retrieve information on manatee distribution, mortality, and feeding areas, as well as migration data collected by a variety of different organizations. GIS can also store information about human use of the waterways, accumulating figures on the frequency of boating and fishing activity in certain areas, and tracking changes in areas of new development. The program can then generate a series of overlay maps that pinpoint exact locations of this data. Ross Wilcox, an ecologist who is grant coordinator of the Center for Environmental Studies at Florida Atlantic University, says this information is invaluable in planning management strategies. In explaining how the system works, Leslie Ward, a marine research associate at Florida's Department of Environmental Protection's Marine Mammal Institute, said,

A researcher can input queries such as "show me all the manatees in a specific area; show me where dead manatees were found in August 1998; or show me the most used feeding grounds in St. Lucie County." GIS helps us visualize a large volume of data much more efficiently than if we had a pile of individual paper maps. With GIS, we can coordinate all the information at one time.[46]

Since much of the danger to sirenians comes from human activity, information gathered by researchers does little good unless there is cooperation from the general public.

Public awareness and education

If manatees and dugongs are to be protected, it is necessary to get the word out that they are endangered; the human-related activities that endanger sirenians must be publicized as well. For example, boaters can be made aware of the practices that can put sirenians at peril and advised as to less-damaging alternatives.

This boater may be unintentionally harming a manatee by scrubbing algae from its hide.

Similarly, people need to learn what to do if they encounter a sirenian or see one that appears to be in distress. Few people realize that specialized knowledge is necessary to provide food or water to a manatee without harming the creature. As the U.S. Fish and Wildlife Service advises:

> Even when well-intentioned, public feeding or watering of wild manatees may alter natural behavior in ways that ultimately change manatee distribution patterns or place wild animals at risk. For example, it may condition animals to approach boats or areas that are hazardous, or encourage them to remain in areas during seasons that could expose them to thermal stress.[47]

Another advantage of public awareness is that, once people are aware of sirenians and their needs, they are more apt to support conservation programs and vote to fund money for the acquisition and maintenance of habitat, for research, and for rehabilitation of injured and sick animals.

Organizations involved in manatee protection devote much of their time and effort toward reaching the public through programs in the schools, posters, pamphlets, brochures, films, and public service announcements in the media. Marine parks and aquariums bring people and manatees together. In Florida, citizens can order special manatee license plates for their vehicles, which both helps raise manatee awareness and provides funds for protection programs. The Save the Manatee Club's Adopt-A-Manatee™ program provides an opportunity for groups or individuals to become personally involved in manatee conservation.

Just as there is a public outreach in the United States concerning manatees, other countries also have public education and awareness programs to promote maintenance and protection of their sirenian populations. In 1984, a number of manatees were brought to Brazil's first hydroelectric reservoir. Their presence at the reservoir, together with an advertising campaign, helped raise public awareness of Amazonian manatees, which are in particular peril because of rain forest loss.

An observation station was set up in Trinidad in 1994 after someone witnessed a local villager slice up a manatee to sell the meat. Following an intensive public education

Funds from the sale of special license plates like this one are contributed to manatee protection efforts.

effort, it was reported that "Hunters in the village have since been reformed and drafted into the conservation project. Since implementation of the project, no harpoonings were reported, but instead a slow growth in the small manatee population."[48] This is what public awareness is all about: One man on a Caribbean island saw a manatee being butchered and objected publicly. Then concerned Trinidadians joined together to start an effective manatee protection program. Raised public awareness, in turn, created its own positive feedback, since well-informed individuals are more likely to spot and report sirenians in trouble, and to insist on enforcement of newly established conservation measures.

Rescue and rehabilitation

In Florida, when an injured manatee is sighted by a citizen, it is reported to the closest rescue agency, which sends a specially trained team to rescue the animal and, if necessary, to transport it to an approved rehabilitation facility for medical treatment. Ann Spellman of the Florida Department of Environmental Protection's Threatened Species Program, says each rescue is unique and calls for on-the-spot decisions and often, makeshift methods of rescue. She has helped to rescue manatees that have been hit by boats, entangled in crab traps or fishing line, caught in drain pipes, and manatees that have become sick from cold stress, stranded, orphaned, and other unpredictable circumstances.

Shawn and Christine

In one rescue, Spellman was called when two children in Cocoa Beach near Cape Kennedy on the east coast of Florida, spotted a manatee trapped in a drainpipe in February 1998. The diameter of the pipe was only thirty-six inches. Nonetheless, Spellman and an assistant crawled in and were surprised to discover a second manatee farther down the pipe. Both manatees had to be moved to a place in the pipe where a storm grate would allow them to be hoisted to ground level. Spellman and her assistant rolled the first manatee onto a stretcher, pulled it about ten feet, and then

This manatee was one of two rescued from a drainpipe in Cocoa Beach, Florida, in February 1998.

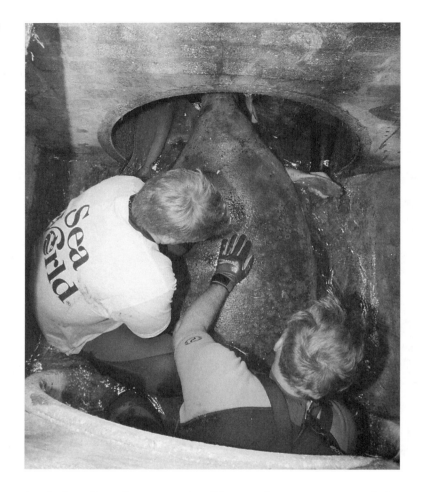

tended to the other manatee. Due to the narrowness of the pipe and the large size of the manatee, the normal stretcher could not be used. Instead, a large piece of plastic sheeting was slipped under the animal to enable the rescuers to slide her backward to the grate. For three hours, Spellman and her assistant crawled among bugs, crabs, fish, and black widow spiders, through the hot, dark, slimy pipe. The water sometimes reached to their knees and other times to their chins. But both manatees were successfully rescued and sent to Sea World in Orlando for treatment and recovery. The animals, named Shawn and Christine for the children who found them, did well at Sea World and were released back to the wild in April 1998.

The rescue of Shawn and Christine was the second manatee rescue from the same pipe within a two-week period. After these incidents, the U.S. Fish and Wildlife Service ordered the city of Cocoa Beach to put a manatee barrier at the storm drain outlet. The city complied within twenty-four hours. The children who found the manatees were given lifetime memberships in Save the Manatee Club, tickets to Sea World, plaques from the city of Cocoa Beach, and letters of recognition from the Department of Environmental Protection.

Not all rescues end happily

Another of Spellman's rescue attempts did not have such a happy ending. In October 1996, some children playing on a riverbank in Melbourne, a few miles south of Cocoa Beach, saw a man intentionally steer his boat over a manatee. A nine-year-old girl said the man steering the boat tried to hit the animal for ten minutes, then finally rode over the animal's back, at which time the boater and his four passengers laughed hysterically. "I kept yelling at them, 'Don't hurt the manatee; don't hurt the manatee, and they just said bad words to me,"[49] the girl said. The incident was reported to the Florida Department of Environmental Protection.

Two days later, Spellman received a call about an injured manatee in the same area. When Spellman arrived, the manatee was not moving its tail and seemed unable to submerge. Not wanting to alarm the animal by using a net, the rescuers followed in a boat until their quarry swam into a closed canal where Spellman was able to approach and make an examination. At least a dozen propeller gashes had slashed the manatee's back and chest. Some of the injuries appeared deep enough to have cut the spinal cord. One rib was severed and could be seen through one of the gashes. Because the

This manatee was mortally injured by a boat that intentionally ran over it in Melbourne, Florida, in October 1996.

animal was no longer bleeding, Spellman judged the injuries to be at least two days old and suspected this was the manatee that had been run over by the boat.

Though the rescue had been successful, the manatee died within a short time. A necropsy showed that the animal was a female around thirty years old that had recently given birth. Other than her injuries, she had been in good health and could have lived another forty years. A dead calf was later found in the area, but whether it had belonged to the dead manatee was not known. The town citizens were outraged at this deliberate killing of a manatee and donated over $15,000 to the arrest and conviction of the boat operator and passengers, but they were never caught.

Timing of a rescue is important. This is particularly true with severe injuries and with animals suffering from cold stress. The longer the animal remains unattended, the less its chances for survival. The main objective in rehabilitating sirenians is to return them to the wild, but, sometimes, this is impossible. If the animal has been too severely injured to survive on its own, it is kept at a marine park.

Role of marine zoos and aquariums

In the United States, and in most other countries today, only sirenians that are being treated for injury or illness or being studied for research may be kept in captivity. And only marine zoos and aquariums have the facilities necessary to allow such treatment and study under humane conditions. Another important function of aquariums is to provide an opportunity for the public to view the animals. Aquariums also help to educate the public about the animals and their needs.

In the early 1980s, a plan was proposed to breed captive manatees and later to release the offspring to the wild in hopes of boosting the diminishing manatee population in Florida.

Raised in captivity—released to the wild

To initiate this program, elaborate plans were made for the release of Sunrise and Savannah, two orphaned mana-

Snooty, the Oldest Captive Manatee

In 1948, a male calf was born to an injured manatee that had been brought to the Miami Seaquarium late in her pregnancy. The mother's injuries were severe and she died within a few months. However, her calf, Snooty, thrived. When he was around a year old, he was moved to a small zoo in Bradenton, Florida, near Tampa. For the next seventeen years, he lived alone in a small tank. Snooty introduced many people to manatees and became the zoo's favorite attraction. Today, Snooty still lives at the zoo in Bradenton, but now swims in a sixty-thousand-gallon tank and has a companion, Newton. At fifty years old, Snooty is the oldest living manatee in captivity. He eats fifty pounds of lettuce, vegetables, and fruit at each of his four meals a day, and particularly likes pineapples and strawberries. He also seems to like women who wear perfume and hauls himself up onto the edge of his pool to get better sniffs.

tees that were being raised at Miami Seaquarium. When they were judged old enough, they were taken to Homosassa Springs Nature World in northwestern Florida. There, they were released into a protected area of the springs where they remained for almost two years. When it was thought they were able to fend for themselves, they were fitted with radio transmitters and set free. Their radio tags were lost within two weeks and the transmitters were found a few months later. No sightings of either manatee were ever reported and no one knows what happened to them. Other experiments also failed, and the breeding program was dropped.

Daryl Domning and several other manatee experts agree that breeding sirenians is not the way to boost their populations. Sirenians born in the wild spend two or more years actively learning how to survive from their mothers. Those born in captivity are deprived of this long training period. They are inexperienced, not only in finding appropriate food, but in swimming in areas with boats and other hazards and in learning travel routes to warmer waters when the weather turns cold. Another reason captive breeding is impractical is the sirenians' slow rate of reproduction. Adding significant numbers to the population would take decades.

Attempts to breed sirenians in captivity and release them to the wild have not been successful.

As Domning has said, "The key to survival of manatees in the wild is to reduce direct mortality due to human activities, as well as to maintain critical habitat."[50]

Protecting sirenian habitat

Habitat is preserved by establishing and maintaining sanctuaries where manatees are protected and public education programs are conducted. When possible, areas that contain critical manatee habitats are purchased by federal or state governments to ensure that those areas will remain undeveloped.

To adequately provide for sirenians' needs, habitats must contain sufficient vegetation and access to freshwater; secluded areas for mating, bearing, and nursing young; resting areas; safe travel corridors connecting habitat areas; and warm-water refuges during cold weather. The challenge to conservationists is to provide the essential habitats, while at the same time making provisions for human needs such as boating, fishing, and coastal development.

The effort to reduce the number of animals injured or killed from collisions with boats includes the posting of low-speed and no-wake zones in areas used by the animals. Enforcement of the posted limits is essential to the plan's success. Safety shrouds around propellers are encouraged for large craft such as tugs and cargo vessels to prevent manatees from being pulled into the blades by their turbulence. Studies are being conducted to evaluate the use of prop guards for small craft as well, but the guard itself can injure the animals in collisions. Further research and development of better guards is needed. Also, some manatees are crushed when caught between two large vessels or between vessels and wharves. Fenders are recommended to reduce these incidents.

Sirenians are often caught and drowned in shrimping and fishing nets. Brochures are distributed to shrimpers advising them of measures they can take to reduce this problem, such as using excluder devices or reducing the amount of towing time, and retrieving the nets as soon as a heavy object is caught.

Many sirenians are injured by foreign objects in the water. They are snagged by lures and hooks. Necropsies disclose rubber bands, cellophane, fishing line, stockings, plastic bags, metal wire, fishhooks, and other discarded trash in the stomachs of retrieved carcasses. Flippers and flukes often become entangled in fishing line or crab trap line, which can result in infections, sometimes causing the loss of the limb or death.

Many manatees in Florida swim in areas where there are flood control gates and canal locks. It is not uncommon for animals to be trapped or crushed when the gates or locks open or close. In the early 1980s gate openings were widened to allow manatees to pass through easily. Other gate areas were fenced. Even more effective is the attachment to the gates of automatic reversal devices, which work much like elevator doors that will not close if a person is in the door's path. Still another safety measure is the installation of sonar devices on the gates that detect the presence of manatees in close proximity. The sonar signal would

Posting speed-control signs and encouraging the use of propeller guards are two ways to limit the injury of manatees by boats.

activate a mechanism that would prevent the gate from closing until the manatee was no longer present. As a result of these measures, manatee deaths due to floodgates and navigation locks have declined.

Have conservation programs worked?

Not all conservation programs meet with widespread public approval, especially when special interests are affected. The fishing and boating industries are often in direct opposition to manatee conservationists when it comes to limiting access to certain areas, regulating speeds, or

Fishermen and boaters claim that there are already too many areas that are made off-limits to them by manatee conservation efforts.

building marinas. Boaters argue that there are already too many regulations against boaters, and that most boaters do not speed in manatee areas. Developers of residential and commercial real estate also balk at restrictions against building new boat docks and dredging canals. Those opposing conservation measures claim that the number of sirenian deaths attributed to human causes and the ruinous effects of development on sea grass beds are exaggerated, that implementation of suggested safety measures would be prohibitively expensive, and that fewer construction projects would mean fewer jobs and higher unemployment.

In 1996, the Australian federal environment minister, Senator Robert Hill, announced the establishment of a series of dugong sanctuaries, laws prohibiting fishing practices that may harm dugongs, and more enforcement of existing laws against the use of mesh fishing nets.

Helene Marsh, one of the world's leading dugong experts, applauded Hill's announcement. "The initiative takes into account the best available scientist advice on dugongs and seagrass and represents a significant step toward halting the decline in dugong numbers. . . . We look forward to action on other causes of the decline especially the conservation of seagrass."[51]

Jeremy Tagar, North Queensland Conservation Council coordinator, said the sanctuaries and protections are good, but that these protections alone would not save the dugong. "The reality is there is no new protection from human threats to dugongs in these areas. Gill netting, hunting, coastal development, vessel traffic and even the use of explosives (for fishing) will continue in the proposed protection areas."[52]

Controversy over dugong regulations also raged in Thailand, where a 1993 ban was recently reversed against the use of fishing nets less than 1.86 miles from shore and restricting large boats from fishing in shallow water.

However, in spite of this opposition, most of the people in sirenian conservation feel that the various programs have helped. Jim Reid of the Sirenia Project in Gainesville, Florida, said, "Manatees in Florida are better off in 1998 than they were 20 years ago because of a combination of factors: the awareness and education programs, more and better management of sanctuaries."[53]

Two Florida Department of Fish and Game officers patrol a manatee habitat.

And Nancy Sadusky of Save the Manatee Club says, "There is a lot more awareness of manatees and the need to protect them today than in the past, but there are certain segments of the population that need the laws to keep them in check. More enforcement on the water would be beneficial."[54]

Priorities in current conservation programs

As for current priorities in programs to save sirenians, particularly the manatees in Florida, one of the major needs appears to be better coordination and cooperation among the many organizations and agencies involved. Ecologist Ross Wilcox cites the need for better administration and management, better enforcement of current protective laws, and more research to advance knowledge of manatee life.

Bob Turner, who works with the U.S. Fish and Wildlife Service Manatee Recovery Plan, confirms that boat mortality is reduced from previous years, but agrees with Sadusky that more patrol officers are needed.

Epilogue

MANATEE SPECIALIST JIM REID expresses concern for the future of sirenians. He points out that environmental conditions of many of Florida's lakes and rivers are very different today than they were fifty years ago. This is solely due to human activity. The changes will be even greater fifty years from now. "Baby manatees born today must continue to have safe places in which to swim 50 years from now or there will be no more manatees."[55] This is true, not only for manatees in Florida, but for all sirenians.

Ross Wilcox urges setting realistic and sustainable goals in conservation instead of going for perfection. "There is going to be runoff from sewers, drainage, fertilizers," he says. "This cannot be stopped or avoided. But this water can be treated before it enters the ocean so that it does not pollute and so the fertilizer runoff is cleaned of the elements that promote the growth of organisms which inhibit the growth of sea grasses."[56]

All experts agree that there is still much to learn about habitat protection, planning, law enforcement, and education. Results of intensive surveys and studies have identified several areas in which sirenian protection can be improved. Federal and state governments should be encouraged to acquire shoreline property and to create a system of sanctuaries and refuges in which human activity would be prohibited or severely limited. Improved enforcement of boating regulations might be achieved through a course that would issue a certificate, through licensing boat operators, and through laws that would enable officials to punish repeat offenders by suspending their licenses.

Humans must improve their understanding of how manatees and dugongs live if the sirenians are to survive. They must also limit or prohibit the activities that are harmful to these mammals.

Suggestions for solving some of the problems

Problems already caused by coastal development could be alleviated by limiting the building of new marinas, ship terminals, boat ramps, and launches in manatee areas. Helpful, as well, would be a requirement for developers who destroy habitats in one area to restore or protect habitats in another to compensate.

On the positive side, the large amount of information and data gathered by several organizations and agencies could be put to better use by expanded and improved use of the geographic information system (GIS) capabilities.

Among all the problems faced by sirenian conservationists, probably one of the biggest is funding. Research, conservation of habitat, rescue and rehabilitation of injured and sick animals, and everything else that is necessary to protect sirenians from possible extinction, is expensive. For example, recovering and studying manatee carcasses after the 1996 red tide in Florida cost millions of dollars. Money used for this purpose had to be diverted from funds designated for other programs.

Tim Dietz said about the Florida manatee,

> The plight of the manatee is as much a story of survival of the Florida ecosystem as it is of the battle to save a single species. For the individuals who keep watch on the dissolution of a fragile environment, the urgency grows daily, the task becomes ever greater and more imposing. But they, like scores of other marine scientists and committed conservationists, maintain a clear vision, a certain hope that transcends the gloom of reality, illuminating a path for a future where answers will be found.[57]

Notes

Introduction

1. Quoted in John E. Reynolds III and Daniel K. Odell, *Manatees and Dugongs.* New York: Facts On File, 1991, p. 135.
2. Reynolds and Odell, *Manatees and Dugongs,* p. 36.

Chapter 1: Manatees—Gentle Giants of the Sea

3. Quoted in Tim Dietz, *The Call of the Siren: Manatees and Dugongs.* Golden, CO: Fulcrum Publishing, 1992, p. 2.
4. Daniel S. Hartman, *Ecology and Behavior of the Manatee (Trichechus Manatus) in Florida.* Pittsburgh, PA: American Society of Mammologists, 1979.
5. Reynolds and Odell, *Manatees and Dugongs,* p. 42.
6. Reynolds and Odell, *Manatees and Dugongs,* p. 40.
7. Quoted in S. H. Ridgeway and Richard J. Harrison, eds., *Handbook of Marine Mammals: The Sirenians and Baleen Whales.* New York: Academic Press, 1985.
8. Quoted in Peter James Spielmann, "Endangered Dugongs," *Soundnet: The Newsletter of the Oceania Project,* October 27, 1997. www.nor.com.au/community/oceania/index.html.
9. Reynolds and Odell, *Manatees and Dugongs,* p. 38.

Chapter 2: Sirenian Behavior

10. Wayne Hartley, ranger at Blue Springs State Park, Volusia County, FL, interview by author, March 12, 1998.
11. Reynolds and Odell, *Manatees and Dugongs,* p. 43.
12. Ann Perry, marine biologist, Florida Department of Environmental Protection, interview by author, March 9, 1998.
13. Dietz, *The Call of the Siren,* p. 29.
14. Reynolds and Odell, *Manatees and Dugongs,* p. 54.
15. Jim Reid, biologist, Sirenia Project, interview by author, March 9, 1998.

16. Lynn Lefebvre, Fact Sheet on Chessie, October 24, 1996. http://biology-usgs.gov/pr/factsheet/chessie.html.

Chapter 3: Sirenia—Prey of Humans

17. Quoted in Warren Zeiller, *Introducing the Manatee.* Gainesville: University of Florida Press, 1992, p. 119.
18. Quoted in Dietz, *The Call of the Siren,* p. 71.
19. Zeiller, *Introducing the Manatee,* p. 122.
20. Quoted in Zeiller, *Introducing the Manatee,* p. 122.
21. Ben Cropp, "Timeless Hunters," *Oceans,* November 1982, p. 20.
22. Quoted in Zeiller, *Introducing the Manatee,* p. 81.
23. Quoted in Zeiller, *Introducing the Manatee,* p. 80.
24. Quoted in Reynolds and Odell, *Manatees and Dugongs,* p. 124.
25. Interview, Jim Reid.
26. Quoted in Dietz, *The Call of the Siren,* p. 69.
27. Cropp, "Timeless Hunters," p. 20.
28. *SireNews,* "Manatee Poaching Continues in Belize," April 1997, p. 6. http://pegasus.cc.ucf.edu/~smm/snews.htm.

Chapter 4: Human Encroachments into Sirenian Environments

29. Reynolds and Odell, *Manatees and Dugongs,* p. 109.
30. R. Reeves, Stewart S. Brent, and Stephen Leatherwood, *The Sierra Club Handbook on Seals and Sirenians.* San Francisco: Sierra Club Books, 1992, p. 288.
31. *Florida Manatee Recovery Plan.* Atlanta: U.S. Fish and Wildlife Service, Southeast Region, 1996, p. 4.
32. Bonnie Bilyeu Gordon, "The Boating Wars," *Sea Frontiers,* March/April 1994, p. 5.
33. Quoted in Jon R. Luoma, "What's Killing the Manatees?" *Audubon,* July/August 1996, pp. 18–21.
34. Quoted in Spielmann, "Endangered Dugongs."
35. Greg Roberts, "Disaster for Dugongs as Nets Take Their Toll," *Sydney (Australia) Morning Herald,* June 10, 1997.
36. Spielmann, "Endangered Dugongs."
37. Reeves, *The Sierra Club Handbook,* p. 289.
38. Spielmann, "Endangered Dugongs."
39. Quoted in Spielmann, "Endangered Dugongs."

40. Quoted in Monica Michael Willis, "Swimming with Manatees: Will Allowing Humans to Interact with These Animals Help or Hurt This Endangered Species?" *Country Living,* November 1997, pp. 29–31.

41. Interview, Jim Reid.

42. Quoted in Willis, "Swimming with Manatees," p. 29.

43. *Manatee News Quarterly,* "Manatee Deaths in Florida," October–December 1997, pp. 3–4.

Chapter 5: Saving Sirenians

44. Reynolds and Odell, *Manatees and Dugongs,* pp. xii–xiii.

45. Interview, Jim Reid.

46. Leslie Ward, marine research associate at the Marine Research Institute, Florida Department of Environmental Protection, interview by author, August 3, 1998.

47. *Florida Manatee Recovery Plan,* p. 91.

48. Celia Sankar, "The Manatee's Hidden Haven," *Americas* (English edition), November/December 1994, p. 2.

49. Quoted in Maurice Tamman, "Boater Steered Right for Manatee," *Florida Today,* October 23, 1996, p. A1+.

50. Quoted in Reynolds and Odell, *Manatees and Dugongs,* p. 164.

51. Robert Hill, Australian senator, minister for the environment, "Dugong Sanctuaries 'A World First,'" August 15, 1997. www.environment.gov.au/portfolio/minister/env/97/mr15aug97.html.

52. Marine Mammals Research and Conservation (MARMAM), "Conservationists Criticize Emergency Measures," December 4, 1996. www.escribe.com/science/marmam/msg00072.html.

53. Interview, Jim Reid.

54. Nancy Sadusky, interview by author, March 11, 1998.

Epilogue

55. Interview, Jim Reid.

56. Ross Wilcox, grant coordinator for Center for Environmental Studies and certified senior ecologist through Ecology Society of America, interview by author, March 15, 1998.

57. Dietz, *The Call of the Siren,* p. 153.

Glossary

aboriginal: Describing the original inhabitants of an area as opposed to those who come from other places to colonize the area.

algae: Plantlike organisms that grow on rocks and other hard surfaces long immersed in water.

aphrodisiac: A substance said to heighten sexual desire.

apprentice: One who learns by working with an experienced, skilled person; this period of instruction is called apprenticeship.

aquatic: Describing plants or animals that live in water.

biology: The study of the life processes of an animal.

blubber: A thick layer of fat between the skin and body organs that protects most sea mammals from cold.

bone marrow: A soft tissue that occupies the cavities of most mammalian bones.

brackish: Describing areas that contain both freshwater and salt water.

carcass: A dead body.

commercial hunting: Hunting done on a large scale with the intent of selling the catch for profit.

contaminants: Substances that pollute the air, water, earth, or other components of an environment.

deforestation: The action or process of clearing forests, especially to make way for new agriculture or construction.

dinghy: A small boat.

dredge: To deepen a waterway with digging machines.

drought: Period when no rain falls.

dugong: A species of Sirenia found in the Indian and Pacific Ocean areas.

ecosystem: A network of interrelated organisms and their environment functioning as an ecological unit in nature.

erosion: The wearing away of soil through wind and water.

estrus: The time when female mammals are ready to mate.

etiology: Cause of disease.

extinct: No longer existing.

fenders: Bumpers or other devices used to lessen the impact of a boat against a manatee.

flippers: The pectoral (side) forelimbs or paddles of marine mammals.

flukes: The two parts of some aquatic mammals' tails.

fossil: A remnant, impression, or trace of an organism of a past geologic age that has been preserved in rock or the earth's crust.

gestation: Period of pregnancy.

gill net: A large mesh net used to catch fish.

habitat: The place or environment where a plant or animal normally lives and grows.

herbivore: Plant-eating animal.

herd: A congregation of animals.

hypothermia: A condition resulting from exposure to extreme cold.

immune system: The bodily system that protects the body from disease.

incidental hunting: Catching one animal in the pursuit of another.

ingest: Eat.

instincts: An inherited tendency of an organism to make a complex and specific response to its environmental conditions without thought.

invertebrates: Organisms lacking a spinal cord, or backbone.

leviathan: A whale or any large sea animal.

malnutrition: The state of insufficient food and nutrients to sustain life.

mammal: Animals that breathe air, give birth to live young, nurse their young, have backbones, and grow body hair.

marina: A dock or basin providing secure moorings for pleasure boats and often offering supply, repair, and other facilities.

marine: Having to do with the sea.

microorganism: An organism of microscopic or ultra-microscopic size.

mixira: Manatee meat cooked and preserved in its own oil.

monofilament line: Nylon or plastic fishing line.

necropsy: An autopsy performed on an animal.

nictitating membrane: A thin membrane found in many vertebrates beneath the lower eyelid that protects the eye from water.

order: A taxonomic group of related organisms that ranks between a family and a class; comes above a species.

physiology: The study of organs, tissues, or cells.

pollutants: Foreign substances that make the air or water unsafe or poison the earth.

predator: An animal that kills and eats other animals.

prey: An animal taken by a predator for food.

refuge: A place that provides shelter or protection.

rehabilitation: The process of restoring to health.

rhizomes: Part of the root system of a plant.

rostral disk: The flattened part of a dugong's snout.

runoff: Wastewater that drains into waterways.

salinity: The amount of salt in the ocean or other body of salt water.

sanctuary: A refuge for wildlife where predators are controlled and hunting is illegal.

scurvy: A disease caused by lack of vitamin C; symptoms include weakness, anemia, bleeding gums, and loosened teeth.

sea grasses: Any of several varieties of grasses that grow under water.

sediment: Drifting dirt and sand that settles on the ocean floor or a river bottom.

Sirenia: The scientific order that includes all manatees and dugongs.

species: A scientific classification of organisms; animals of the same species can breed with one another.

substance hunting: Hunting done by a small group of people who keep and eat the meat.

taxonomist: A scientist specializing in the naming and classifying of species.

taxonomy: A scientific system of classifying and naming groups of animals.

teats: The mammary glands or nipples of a mammal used for nursing its young.

thermal stress: The result of being exposed to cold water (in Sirenia, water below 68 degrees Fahrenheit).

toxins: Poisonous substances.

transmitter: An electronic device that emits a continuous radio signal.

transponder: An electronic device that beeps when scanned with a special "reader."

VHF: Very high frequency.

viable: Capable of living successfully for an extended period of time.

Organizations
to Contact

Army Corps of Engineers (ACOE)
Jacksonville District
Public Affairs Office
P.O. Box 4970
Jacksonville, FL 32232
(904) 232-2234

A federal agency that oversees water resource development in rivers, lakes, harbors, and wetlands. This agency is responsible for maintaining harbors and navigation channels, including the Intracoastal Waterway, a major migration corridor for manatees.

Blue Springs State Park
2100 W. French Ave.
Orange City, FL 32763
(904) 775-3663

Blue Springs State Park is a winter refuge near Orlando, Florida, where the warm springs maintain a temperature of 72 degrees year round. Wayne Hartley is the ranger, and many of the manatees who winter here are part of Save the Manatee Club's adoption program. (See p. 99.)

Convention of International Trade in Endangered Species of Wild Fauna and Flora (CITES)
CITES Secretariat
15, chemin des Anémones
CH-1219 Châtelaine-Genève, Switzerland
(+4122) 979 9139, 979 9140
fax: (+4122) 797 3417
e-mail: cites@unep.ch

CITES is an organization of 103 countries that provides a framework for regulating trade in plants and animals that either are or may be threatened with extinction.

Crystal River National Wildlife Refuge
1502 SE Kings Bay Dr.
Crystal River, FL 34429
(352) 563-2088
e-mail: R4RW_FL.CHS@FWS.gov
Crystal River National Wildlife Refuge, on the west coast of Florida about sixty miles north of Tampa, is a manatee sanctuary set up by the National Wildlife Refuge system, a department of the U.S. Fish and Wildlife Service.

Epcot's Living Seas
Disney World
Lake Buena Vista, FL 32830
(407) 560-7688

Part of Disney World, Epcot's Living Seas provides the public with an excellent aquarium and has a manatee rehabilitation and research facility.

Florida Audubon Society (FAS)
1331 Palmetto Ave., Suite 110
Winter Park, FL 32789
(407) 539-5700
website: http://www.audubon.usf.edu

The Florida Audubon Society is Florida's oldest and largest conservation organization. FAS provides information and education services on environmental issues and endangered species.

Florida Department of Environmental Protection Headquarters (FDEP)
Bureau of Protected Species Management
3900 Commonwealth Blvd.
MS 245
Tallahassee, FL 32399-3000
(850) 922-4330
website: www.dep.state.fl.us/

The FDEP, as the watchdog for Florida's natural resources, works to protect, conserve, and manage Florida's environment and natural resources. One of the FDEP's responsibilities is rescuing injured manatees.

Florida Department of Natural Resources (DNR)

Office of Protected Species Management
3900 Commonwealth Blvd. R321
Tallahassee, FL 32399
(904) 922-4330

The DNR works in conjunction with the U.S. Fish and Wildlife Service, the Florida Department of Environmental Protection, and the Florida Game and Freshwater Fish Commission to protect manatees and to rescue injured manatees.

Florida Game and Freshwater Fish Commission

Endangered Species Coordinator
Farris Bryant Building
620 S. Meridian St.
Tallahassee, FL 32301
(800) 342-9620 (Call this number to report wildlife law violations.)
(904) 488-3831 (Use this number for all other purposes.)

Florida's agency responsible for management of the state's wildlife and freshwater fisheries resources. Coordinates with USFWS's programs. Operates the WILDLIFE ALERT program that provides rewards to citizens reporting wildlife law violations in Florida.

Florida Office of Environmental Education

3900 Commonwealth Blvd.
MS 30
Tallahassee, FL 32399-3000
(850) 922-4330
website: www.dep.state.fl.us/

Another branch of FDEP, this one responsible for environmental control such as water quality, wetlands development regulation, pollution control, solid waste and recycling, and location of power plants.

Florida Power and Light Company
Environmental Affairs Dept.
P.O. Box 088801
North Palm Beach, FL 33408-8801
(800) 552-8440

Florida's largest electric utility company. Five of its plants provide winter refuges for manatees. The company contributes to manatee research, conducts public awareness information programs, and provides viewing areas where the public can watch the manatees while they are in the refuges.

Homosassa Springs State Park (refuge)
9225 West Fishbowl Dr.
P.O. Box 189
Homosassa Springs, FL 32647
(904) 628-5343
website: www.dep.state.fl.us/parks/HomosassaSprings/
homosassa.html

Homosassa Springs State Park, a facility of the Florida Department of Environmental Protection, houses a manatee research and rehabilitation site for manatees that have been orphaned or injured in the wild and also for manatees that have been born in captivity. Public viewing from underwater viewing areas is provided along with programs to promote public awareness and education about manatees.

Lowry Park Zoological Garden
7530 North Blvd.
Tampa, FL 33604-4700
(813) 935-8552

A manatee rehabilitation facility offering year-round care and public viewing of manatees. The Manatee Hotline, 800-DIAL-FMP, is the number to call to report a manatee that appears to be injured, trapped, or otherwise in danger.

Miami Seaquarium
4400 Rickenbacker Causeway
Miami, FL 33149
(305) 351-5707

A research and rehabilitation facility for manatees that also provides educational programs and public viewing.

Save the Manatee Club
500 N. Maitland Ave., Suite 210
Maitland, FL 32751
(800) 432-5646
e-mail: manatee@america.com
website: www.objectlinks.com/manatee

Established in 1981 by singer Jimmy Buffet and former Florida governor Bob Graham, Save the Manatee Club promotes public awareness and education about manatees. The club sponsors the Adopt-a-Manatee program, in which individuals or groups can adopt one of the manatees that winter at Homosassa Springs State Park (see p. 98). Call the number above for information on how to adopt a manatee.

Sea World of Florida
7007 Sea World Dr.
Orlando, FL 32809
(407) 363-2355 • (407) 363-3600

One of Florida's foremost manatee research and rehabilitation centers. Also has public viewing areas.

Sirenia Project
412 NE 16th Ave., Room 250
Gainesville, FL 32601
(904) 372-2571

This program, administered under the National Biological Service of the USFWS, conducts field research on manatee biology, tracks east-coast Florida manatees, and participates in salvaging dead manatees and rehabilitating injured ones.

United States Fish and Wildlife Service (USFWS)
Wildlife Enhancement Field Office
Manatee Coordinator
6620 Southpoint Dr. South, Suite 231
Jacksonville, FL 32216
(904) 232-2580

A federal program that operates under the Department of the Interior and is the primary agency concerned with conservation of the nation's wildlife. USFWS operates many subdepartments, each with its own responsibilities in protecting and saving Florida manatees. Sponsor of the Sirenia Project based at the University of Florida at Gainesville.

World Conservation Union
Ave. du Mont-Blanc
CH-1196 Gland
Switzerland
This organization publishes the CITES Red Data Books.

Suggestions for Further Reading

Books

Margaret Goff Clark, *The Vanishing Manatee.* New York: Cobblehill Books, 1990. Illustrated with photos. Describes the physical characteristics, habitat, and behavior of manatees and dugongs.

Kathy Darling, *Manatee: On Location.* New York: Lothrop, Lee & Shepard, 1991. Photo essay.

Amanda Harman, *Manatees and Dugongs (Endangered).* Tarrytown, NY: Marshall Cavendish, 1997. Illustrated. Good basic information.

Rei Ohara and Akemi Hotta, *Manatee.* San Francisco: Chronicle, 1998. Excellent photos taken at Florida's Crystal River.

Jean H. Sibbald, *The Manatee.* Parsippany, NJ: Silver Burdett, 1996. Discusses the appearance and behavior of the manatee and examines its relationship with humans.

Alvin Silverstein et al., *The Manatee.* Brookfield, CT: Millbrook Press, 1995. Examines the life of the gentle, endangered sea creature, whose unusual appearance has inspired sailors' tales of mermaids and water nymphs over the centuries.

Mary Unterbrink, *Manatees—Gentle Giants in Peril.* St. Petersburg, FL: Great Outdoors Publishing, 1984. More of a pamphlet than a book, but contains good basic information.

Victoria Brook Van Meter, *The West Indian Manatee in Florida.* Miami: Florida Power and Light, 1982. Booklet containing excellent basic information on the Florida manatee.

Websites

America's National Wildlife Refuges (http://refuges:fws.gov/NWRSFiles/WildlifeMgmet/SpeciesAccounts/Mammals/FLManatee/FLMan). Information on the Florida manatee with links to other sites.

Anneberg/CPB Projects page (www.learner.org/aboutacp/#acpbmsproj). Comprehensive site with many links to information on wildlife. Use the link to the Journey North site for information on wildlife migrations, including manatees.

Caribbean Stranding Network (http://netdial.caribe.net/~mignucci/). Gives current information in Spanish on manatees in Central America. Can be translated using AltaVista search engine.

The Chessie Page (www.oceanicresearch.org/chessie.html). Documents progress of Chessie, a manatee who traveled from Florida to Rhode Island.

CITES (www.wcmc.org.uk/cgi-bin/anap97.pl). Provides updates and information on status of all animals protected under the Convention on the Intenational Trade in Endangered Species.

The Dugong Page (http://home.t-online.de/home/rothauscher/dugong.htm). An excellent source containing many links to other sites.

Endangered Species Home Page (www.fws.gov/r9endspp/endspp.html). Information and links to sites covering all endangered species. Special pages for manatees can be accessed from this site.

Florida Caribbean Science Center (www.nfrcg.gov/sirenia/). Information and updates on their work with manatees and other animals.

Florida Department of Environmental Protection, Bureau of Protected Species Management (www.dep.state.fl.us/psm/webpages/manatees/telemtry.htm). Links to pages on manatee information, including rescues, telemetry, and satellite tracking.

Florida Marine Research Institute (www.fmri.usf.edu/manatees.htm). Many links to information about manatees.

Marine Mammals Research and Conservation (MARMAM), "Conservationists Criticize Emerging Measures," December 4, 1996. (www.escribe.com/science/marmam/msg00072.html). An open discussion group (via e-mail) of laypeople and professionals interested in marine mammal conservation.

Save the Manatee Club (www.savethemanatee.org/). Excellent site. Information on Adopt-a-Manatee program, current research on manatees, and places to see them.

SireNews (http://pegasus.cc.ucf.edu/~smm/snews.htm). An electronic newsletter providing international news updates on manatees and dugongs.

Sirenia Project (www.fcsc.usgs.gov/sirenia/index.html). A government program carried out in conjunction with the University of Florida at Gainesville.

Soundnet (www.nor.com.au/community/oceania/index.html). An electronic newsletter providing international information on the status of endangered sea mammals.

U.S. Fish and Wildlife Service, Division of Endangered Species (www.fws.gov/r9endspp/esa.html). Links to information on all endangered wildlife. Gives entire text of Endangered Species Act of 1973.

Works Consulted

Books

Tim Dietz, *The Call of the Siren: Manatees and Dugongs.* Golden, CO: Fulcrum Publishing, 1992. An excellent book, written from the author's personal experience in researching sirenians. Contains many anecdotes and interesting bits of history.

Daniel S. Hartman, *Ecology and Behavior of the Manatee (Trichechus Manatus) in Florida.* Pittsburgh, PA: American Society of Mammologists, 1979. This book is a detailed report of Hartman's long-term study. Excellent primary resource material.

R. Reeves, Stewart S. Brent, and Stephen Leatherwood, *The Sierra Club Handbook on Seals and Sirenians.* San Francisco: Sierra Club Books, 1992. A reference book with short but detailed entries on many facets of sirenian life.

John E. Reynolds III and Daniel K. Odell, *Manatees and Dugongs.* New York: Facts On File, 1991. Written for both the layperson and the professional, this book is considered one of the primary sources of current Sirenia information.

S. H. Ridgeway and Richard J. Harrison, eds., *Handbook of Marine Mammals: The Sirenians and Baleen Whales.* New York: Academic Press, 1985. A reference book containing excellent resource material.

Warren Zeiller, *Introducing the Manatee.* Gainesville: University of Florida Press, 1992. The author, who worked with the Miami Seaquarium for twenty-five years, provides many detailed stories about the manatees treated at the Seaquarium.

Special Reports

Bureau of Protected Species Management, *Florida Manatee Program Review.* Tallahassee: Florida Marine Research Institute, Florida Department of Environmental Protection, Manatee Technical Advisory Council, 1997.

Florida Manatee Recovery Plan. Atlanta: U.S. Fish and Wildlife Service, Southeast Region, 1996.

Thomas J. O'Shea, Bruce B. Ackerman, and H. Franklin Percival, eds., *Population Biology of the Florida Manatee.* Washington, DC: U.S. Department of the Interior, National Biological Service, 1995.

James P. Reid and Thomas J. O'Shea, *Three Years Operational Use of Satellite Transmitters on Florida Manatees: Tag Improvements Based on Challenges from the Field.* Gainesville, FL: U.S. Fish and Wildlife Service Sirenia Project, 1989.

Periodicals

Ben Cropp, "Timeless Hunters," *Oceans,* November 1982.

Daryl P. Domning, "Marching Teeth of the Manatee," *Natural History,* May 1983.

Rhonda Lucas Donald, "Travels of Chessie," *Ranger Rick,* May 1997.

Douglas Faulkner and Jack McClintock, "Too Nice to Live: Manatees Are So Easygoing They Can't Protect Themselves from Their Only Enemy—Man," *Life,* November 1990.

Stephen Frink, "Quicksilver Adventure: Snorkeling with Florida's Manatees," *Skin Diver,* June 1996.

Bonnie Bilyeu Gordon, "The Boating Wars," *Sea Frontiers,* March/April 1994.

Phyllis Hockman, "Manatee Madness," *Insight on the News,* March 24, 1997.

Dan Keipal, "Manatees Pulled from Drain Pipe," *Florida Today,* November 4, 1997.

John Kiely, "A Million Years in the Making," *American Way,* February 1, 1991.

Beth Livermore, "Tracking the Elusive Manatee," *Sea Frontiers,* December 1994.

Jon R. Luoma, "What's Killing the Manatees?" *Audubon,* July/August 1996.

Manatee News Quarterly, "Manatee Deaths in Florida," October–December 1997.

Kathleen McAuliffe, "Saving Manatees: Researchers Take to the Air to Preserve a Threatened Species," *Omni,* October 1993.

Robert McNally, "The Short, Unhappy Saga of Steller's Sea Cow," *Sea Frontiers,* May/June 1984.

Jim Motavalli, "Manatee Mania: Is Florida Loving Its Endangered Marine Mammals to Death?" *Earth Action Network,* March/April 1997.

People Weekly, "Plague at Sea: Scott Wright Searches for What's Ailing the Manatees," April 1, 1996.

Anna Prokos, "Staying Alive: How We're Fighting to Save Endangered Species," *3-2-1 Contact,* June 1997.

Linda M. Rancourt, "Marine Mammoth," *National Parks,* September/October 1996.

J. E. Reynolds, "The Florida Manatee, Myth vs Truth," *Sea Frontiers,* July/August 1976.

Greg Roberts, "Disaster for Dugongs as Nets Take Their Toll," *Sydney (Australia) Morning Herald,* June 10, 1997.

Celia Sankar, "The Manatee's Hidden Haven," *Americas* (English edition), November/December 1994.

Robert Sims, "Manatee Count May Offer Some Help," *Palm Beach Daily News,* January 19, 1997.

Maurice Tamman, "Boater Steered Right for Manatee," *Florida Today,* October 23, 1996.

Leslie Ward and Brad Weigle, "To Save a Species: GIS for Manatee Research and Management," *GIS World, Inc.,* August 1993.

John P. Wiley Jr., "Manatees, like Their Siren Namesakes, Lure Us to the Deep," *Smithsonian,* September 1987.

Monica Michael Willis, "Swimming with Manatees: Will Allowing Humans to Interact with These Animals Help or Hurt This Endangered Species?" *Country Living,* November 1997.

Internet Sources

Iain Christie, "Mozambique Campaigns to Keep Dugong Off the Menu," *Soundnet: The Newsletter of the Oceania Project,* November 24, 1997. www.nor.com.au/users/oceania/soundnet/cover.html.

Robert Hill, Australian senator, minister for the environment, "New Action on Dugong Conservation," March 31, 1997. www.environment.gov.au/portfolio/minister/env/97/mr31mar97.html.

———, "Dugong Sanctuaries 'A World First,'"August 15, 1997. www.environment.gov.au/portfolio/minister/env/97/mr15aug97.html.

———, "Urgent Action Taken on Dugong Decline," December 4, 1996. www.environment.gov.au/portfolio/minister/env/96/mr4dec.html.

Lynn Lefebvre, "Fact Sheet on Chessie," October 24, 1996. http://biology-usgs.gov/pr/factsheet/chessie.html.

Frank Perry, "The Fossil Sea Cow." www.cruzio.com/%7Esclibs/history/spanish/seacow.html.

Anthony Preen, *Soundnet: The Newsletter of the Oceania Project,* "Tribal Hunters to Back Off Dugongs," March 9, 1997. www.nor.com.au/community/oceania/index.html.

SireNews, "Manatee Poaching Continues in Belize," April 1997. http://pegasus.cc.ucf.edu/~smm/snews.htm.

Soundnet: The Newsletter of the Oceania Project, "Ban on Mesh Netting to Protest Endangered Dugongs," June 16, 1997. www.nor.com.au/users/oceania/soundnet/cover.html.

———, "Dugong 3 Brisbane Reopens," June 16, 1997. www.nor.com.au/users/oceania/soundnet/cover.html.

———, "Thailand Environment: Dugongs Threatened by Nets," May 15, 1997. www.nor.com.au/users/oceania/soundnet/cover.html.

———, "War Games Will Hurt Dugong Population Say Greenies," March 4, 1997. www.nor.com.au/users/oceania/soundnet/cover.html.

Peter James Spielmann, "Endangered Dugongs," *Soundnet: The Newsletter of the Oceania Project,* October 27, 1997. www.nor.com.au/community/oceania/index.html.

U.S. Department of the Interior, "Two Female Manatees First to Be Tracked into Puerto Rico," news release, September 12, 1997. http://biology.usgs.gov/pr/newsrelease/1997/9-16.html.

Index

Picture Credits

About the Author

Claire Price-Groff is the author of several books for young adults. Ms. Price-Groff lived in Florida for several years. where she became enamored of the manatee and concerned for its future. She now lives in the mountains of western North Carolina with her husband and their little black dog and orange marmalade kitten.